PAUL GARVEY

FIXERS

GRIT TO GOLD PUBLISHING

Dublin

ISBN-10: 1943415013
ISBN-13: 978-1943415014

Also by Paul Garvey

Blackpool Knights
A Ghost is Born
Rook to Bishop
Green Wings to Eden
Tomorrow's Sun

For Scott Keefe

1

A gunslinger's worst nightmare must be to die with a loaded revolver in his hand. Mine has always been to die with a pen between my fingers and holding an empty notebook. I'm tired of having nightmares and I could die any second now, so I'm going to tell you a story before it's too late.

My name's Rick Sherman. I would've killed for a nickname growing up, well, a good nickname anyway or even an okay one. Slick Rick the rapper took Slick Rick. He took Rick the Ruler too now that I think of it. I wasn't a London gangster, so I felt like Richie didn't fit. I was too average to be Fat Rick or Skinny Ricky or Stretch. Big Dick was my Dad's name, still is actually, wherever the hell he is. He reckons it has very little to do with his name. I reckon it's related to his demeanor rather than any reference to his genitalia. Big Rick was too close to Big Dick, plus, like I said, I'm not that big. The alternative was Little Dick and, well, obviously no way. So it's always just

been Rick or Ricky. On the odd occasion I refer to myself in the third person it's Rick or Richard. A grown man calling himself Ricky doesn't sit right with me. It makes me picture a bassist or drummer from an ageing eighties hair band, scalp on top, but hanging onto threads in the back. You know the look. It's like Hulk Hogan without the bulk. That's enough with the introductions for now, you'll get to know me more as we get into it. Anyway, away we go.

I had an address scribbled on a napkin crumbled in my fist. I got the call at home when I was eating a sandwich and wrote it down on the first thing to hand. Looking at the napkin, I could smell mustard, but couldn't see it. I hate mustard. I don't know how it showed up on my napkin or my sandwich and the stench of it made me nauseous. I checked the address again outside what I thought was a derelict building in an alley that smelled like piss. There was no mistaking it. I was at the right place. I spit my chewed gum into the napkin, balled it up and dropped it into the street. The litter was an improvement. I pushed the door open to the Harlot's Den. I could still smell mustard on my hand and piss in the air. I know what you're thinking, Harlot's Den, it must be a strip club. You're wrong. It's not a strip

club. It is a brothel though. I didn't know that at the time, but I pieced it together quickly. The moment I walked in all I really thought was what a shitty, slimy dive of a bar. I wouldn't want to be caught dead in there and here I was alive walking in.

Inside the piss smell went away, but it was replaced by one of sweat, stale booze and shit. A red tint covered the room which looked to have smoke billowed along the ceiling. At first I thought they must've had a dry ice guy, but it turned out there was just an utter disregard for the smoking ban. The music was loud and bass heavy, it gave me a headache and threw off my sense of balance. It was a cross between rap and electro-house music. It sounded like a Beastie Boys instrumental from the Intergalactic album. I grabbed a bar stool with my hands and put my weight on it for a few seconds to get my balance back. I scanned the room but everything was blurry. Water sprinkled my face and startled me. I turned towards the source to see the bartender dropping her hand back into a glass and flicking her fingers at me. She got me good the second time and it wasn't water, it was whiskey. It stung my eyes and I had to blink the tears out of them. When the blur cleared, the bartender still stood looking at me. Her hair was brown and dirty. She had it to the side and the ponytailed bunch was a ball of frizz. She was bone thin and wore too much make up, or at least too much eye shadow. She mouthed something to me but I couldn't hear her over the music or read her lips. I leaned my ear in. She grabbed it and pulled. It hurt.

'You all right?' She asked.

'Yeah, why?' I said.

'No reason. What do you want?'

'Beer I guess.' I said.

'You guess?'

I kicked it around again and said 'Yeah beer.'

She nodded, grabbed a glass and poured a beer. She slid it over to me. It looked like old piss. I took a sip. It tasted like it too. I must've winced because she frowned and called me a pussy.

'Hey' I yelled over the music. 'I'm here for Big Dick.'

She raised an eyebrow, but didn't answer.

'Wait . . . no.' I said. 'Not . . . I mean Big Dick, the man, you know?'

'As opposed to what?'

'Big Dick.' I said. 'Come on, I know you know him.'

'Not sure what you heard.' She said. 'Pussy, maybe I could help you.'

Hearing the word pussy from this girl's mouth twice in two minutes made me lightheaded and weirdly aroused.

'No, listen.' I said. 'Big Dick, he's my father.'

'Oh.' She said. 'So you're Little Dick?'

I wanted to scream, but I didn't.

'I'm Ricky.' I said, breaking my own rule, it just came out like that.

She made a face, my guess is it was her reaction to a grown man calling himself Ricky. 'Big Dick's around the back.'

'The back I asked?'

'Yeah the back.'

I looked around first, just to look suspicious and asked 'He ain't . . . ya know?' I'd gathered at that stage the bar was more than just a bar. Though I was still thinking strip club at that point.

'His pants are on. There's a bar back there. Take your beer with you, I'm the only one working.' She said.

I nodded and grabbed my glass of piss. It had gone warm too. 'Great.' I thought. I walked through a doorway that had seashell drapes hanging that sounded like falling stones as I pushed past them. The back room was darker and redder, but at least the music was lower, pulsing bass traded in for smooth jazz, although the vibration still made the wall behind the bar shake.

Big Dick sat at the corner of the bar by himself. A beer, a small glass, and a bottle of fireball cinnamon whiskey sat with him. A beige sports jacket stretched tightly over his giant back. He wore a hat that looked tired and old and added years to him. His nose was big and red, made even more so by the unflattering light. His large hands covered much of the pint glass in front of him.

'Dad.' I said, loud enough so he could adjust to my presence. Big Dick isn't a man you want to startle. He's the type to punch first and apologize after. He turned to me and smiled. He raised his hand to wave me over.

'Little Dick.' He yelled. 'What it is!'

I gulped. He knew damn well I loathed that name. He called me by it anyway. Big Dick did things his own way always, often to the detriment of those around him. That's probably why he sat alone drinking his face off in that seedy shit hole. Big Dick was a writer in his day, a journalist. He was considered a very good one. He did investigative journalism, known for breaking big stories, sought after by big name publications and networks. Anytime I had the misfortune of running into an old colleague of his, I had to listen about how Big Dick was Pulitzer Prize material, whatever that was supposed to mean. He was at the top of his game. Then he took some time out and wrote a couple of books. They were big nonfiction pieces, thick and incredibly boring. One flop injured him, the second crippled his confidence. He traded in writing for full-time drinking after that. Since then he looked worse, but seemed to have felt much better. He'd been in much better moods since anyway. He looked haggard and always smelled like shit and cinnamon whiskey, but I got the sense he finally found his passion. Good for him.

About the time he quit writing and started drinking, I stopped working and started writing. I kept drinking too though, I like to keep balanced. At the start, things were looking up. For one, I had the same name as Big Dick, known to the literary consumers as Richard Sherman. The Jr. at the end of my name was inconsequential. Naturally, those in the business figured I was him and even if they knew I wasn't, they knew I was his son and the name alone might sell papers. I wrote freelance, got a decent check off of most of the known titles once. I never saw a second check though from any of them. Only one article ever actually saw it through to final print copy. It was a red top daily. I got a few inches on page twenty five next to a tampon ad and before the sports section. I thought that was me on the upswing, pushing through once and for all, and the first of many breaks. My optimism was short-lived however. It ended the second it became clear that the piece, a Hollywood who's doing who and who's getting fat, was a complete and utter fabrication. The libel lawsuit bankrupted the hundred year-old newspaper. If my name was worth shit at the time, I would've been sunk. But it wasn't, so I wasn't.

'Hi Dad.' I said to him again when I got closer.

'Around here, it's Big Dick son. No Dad in these parts.'

'I am not calling you that.'

'Your mom did.'

'That's fucking disgusting.' I said.

'No it isn't, it's the natural order of things.'

'Whatever Dad, what the hell is this place?'

'This is my little slice of heaven.'

'What do you mean? You own this shit hole?'

'What? No goddamnit.'

'Maybe he does.' The same bartender said, she appeared out of nowhere. 'Through squatters rights I mean.' She looked like a tall lollipop with mascara.

'We're having a conversation.' I told her.

'I know.' She said.

'I think Little Dick wants to talk to his old man alone darling.' Big Dick said.

She disappeared without another word.

'You've offended her now.' He said.

'She'll get over it I'm sure.'

'She will, but she also might not be so generous on my tab.'

'How did you find this dump anyway?' I asked.

'I've been coming here for years. Anytime I was working something and the subject needed to meet discreetly. You know, politicians, businessmen, cops, you name it. We could always meet here, no chance of running into respectables, you know what I'm saying? Only a handful of these places existed back then. Only one does now and you're in it. The yuppie infusion closed most, then the financial crisis took the rest.'

'Shame.' I said.

'It is a goddamn shame. You can leave that

smarmy attitude outside. This city used to have grit. Now look at it, lattes and fucking yoga everywhere.'

'Don't worry Dad, we've still got guns and drugs. There's plenty of crime kicking around yet.'

'Yeah and thank god for that.'

'You ever have a latte?' I asked.

'I've had coffee and I've had milk, I can do the math. I take mine black and whiskey soaked now.'

'Yeah, that and everything else.'

'I've earned it.' Big Dick said.

'I agree, though I'd be surprised if we meant it in the same way.' I looked around for a half second. When I turned back, two full beers sat in front of us.

'She's fast.' Big Dick said when he noticed my surprise. The lack of air inside was suffocating me. My headache wouldn't go away and the poor lighting kept me dizzy and disoriented. I remember feeling like I could faint any second. I pulled over a bar stool and held tight to the worn fabric like a bull rider. I grabbed the piss beer and drank it half down in a gulp to get the effect without really tasting it. I could feel my dad's eyes on me, but he stayed silent. I waited a few seconds then let out a massive belch. The girl appeared from nowhere again darting around the corner like she was shot from a pinball machine. She said nothing, but managed to slow down long enough to pass on a disgusted look.

'Excuse me.' I said. She kept moving.

'She'll come around.' Big Dick said. 'Listen, I'm glad you found the place. You don't look so great.'

'You're talking?' I thought but didn't say. I did say, 'You're note said it was important.'

'No it didn't. It said we should talk. What you inferred is not necessarily what it said. Anyway, I got a call from an old friend . . . a concerned friend.'

'Who is that?'

'Don't matter his name. It was a contact from the *Blackpool Daily*. Well, he was from the *Blackpool Daily*. May Bog rest its soul.'

'Good one.' I said. Then I finished off the rest of my beer in my second gulp.

'That's the best you could do?' Big Dick asked. 'A piece on a B-list wannabe starlet? What happened, bad source?'

I shook my head 'No.'

'You Billy Shakespeared?'

A nod.

'With that shit? Jesus Christ.'

'I needed money.' I pleaded. 'A few months back on the rent. Not my finest hour, I'll admit. I shouldn't have made it up. I figured no one would read that far into the paper. It was page twenty-five with used cars and cats for sale for chrissakes.'

'I don't give a bollocks if you Billy Shakespeared. We all did it. Anything to sell the papers in my day. That was the only thing that mattered. We worried about what was juicy and believable and what could sell papers and get people to stick ads on it. See, we didn't lie so much as create the truth.'

'I don't get it.'

'Considering that shit story you produced, I'm not surprised you can't figure it out.'

'Thanks Dad.'

'Don't mention it.'

'Yeah no problem.'

'No, seriously don't mention I'm your Dad, least don't go out of your way to do so.'

Big Dick was an apt name I thought after he said that.

'Listen kid.' He said. 'We all did it, it's true, but that B-list pile of turd you came up with . . . you once told me you were a writer. Is that right?'

'I guess.' I said.

'Well, a writer's gotta have inspiration. You want to report on a child star going into rehab, join the fucking network news.'

'Like I said Dad, I needed the money.'

'You could've come to me, instead you sunk a newspaper that's been around for over a century. At least you'll probably get a footnote in the history books. Maybe that can be your legacy. We can call you the virus . . . no, the sinker. Hell, people might think you're a ground ball pitcher.' Big Dick said. 'That fucking newspaper outlasted the Great Depression, reported on World War II, the moon landing, fucking Vietnam . . . but you sunk the thing with some made up scribble about absolutely jack shit, some pink shoe and branded t-shirt wearing hipster with abandonment issues and a legal team.'

I felt about the size of a regular M&M when he finished. A peanut M&M would've cast a shadow. 'I think you made your point.' I told him.

'Well then. Good.' Big Dick said. He looked away from me and emptied each glass in front of him down his throat.

'Wait, what did your contact say?' I asked.

'Who?'

'Your buddy, you know, the guy from the Daily. You said you talked to him.'

'Oh yeah, him. He was after me for damages.'

'Damages? What did you do?'

'Me? I didn't do a goddamn thing. He was on the hunt for damages belonging to you.'

'Can they do that?'

'They won't. I told him where to go.'

'I didn't mean to, you know, sink you in it.'

He waved me off with his hand. 'It's my fault.' He said. 'I should've given you a different name.'

Real nice, I thought. I said 'He can't legally take anything from you though?'

'What's left to take? I have nothing but my bollocks and good looks left.'

'Finally, it pays to be poor.' I said.

'Well, maybe not for you.'

'What do you mean?' I asked.

'I mean jail. They want you dragged in, charged with a crime, the whole nine yards.'

'Shit. Can they do that?'

'Did you commit a crime?'

'Probably, maybe, I don't know. Shit.'

'Relax Little Dick. He gave you an out.'

'An out?'

'Yeah, a way out, a settlement.'

'And what's that?'

'You can bring back the *Blackpool Daily*. Get it

up and running, making money, then give it back.'

'How the hell am I supposed to do that? I wouldn't have the slightest idea where to start.'

'You could ask for help.'

I looked at him, the fat, old, worn, drunk, shit-smelling, turd of a man. 'You're gonna help me?' I asked.

He smiled at me. 'If you listen to every fucking word I say, every last detail and follow directions, then yeah I'm gonna help you.'

'Okay.' I said. 'But . . . why?'

'Well Junior. You're my son goddamnit and once you've horsed every flea-infested bag in this place and the tab is long enough to wipe the ass of a giant with the runs, then there just ain't nothing left to do.'

2

I look at elderly people some time and think when did being old become an excuse for not giving a shit about how you treat people? Surely the closer you get to the end, the faster you want to stack the Karma deck in your favor, right? I respect my elders and all that, but only as much as I respect everyone else, at least as a baseline. If anyone is polite or nice to me, I act accordingly in return. I give everyone I meet the same baseline starting point level of polite respect and courtesy. Then I adjust that upwards or downwards depending on that person's reciprocal attitude towards me. I think that's fair. I'm not religious, so the only way I see myself living forever is inside other people's minds, those that bother to remember me that is. So I genuinely aim to give them a positive impression. No one wants to live on as an eternal douche bag. Not me at least. Not if I can avoid it.

Why am I beefing on old people you might ask. Well, Big Dick sent me to some ass-end part of town to meet someone about something. The details were scarce. He said the person would know me, so don't worry about it. He said not to wrap a scarf around my neck or anything romantic like that. He said she'd know me when she saw me. So it was a she. 'Interesting.' I thought. It almost felt like a date. I wore my nicest shirt and my going out sneakers. As you guessed I'm sure, I was between automobiles at the time. I could've kept my last car no problem, all I had to do was commit to living in it. I didn't want to be tied down, so I got rid of it and paid my rent with the proceeds. So instead of shooting across the city in a fine air conditioned automobile, I caught the bus. It felt like the bingo bus. There was either an over eighty rave going on somewhere or these people didn't have anything else to do so they rode public transport back and forth since it was free for pensioners and provided better entertainment than daytime television with its never ending ads for injury lawyers and erection drugs. The bus stopped every five feet. I was standing and holding on to one of those rubber handles that do nothing to keep you firm on the ground. I was swinging like Arnie from a

helicopter the whole time, sweating through my shirt and hip checking old ladies.

I reached over and hit the colored strip to ding the bell for my stop when I recognized the area that Big Dick described. The bus swung to the curb. I wiggled my way to the front and jumped down. I felt better right away with my feet on solid ground and my hips no longer thrusting around like a rodeo clown. The bus steamed away and a waft of diesel smoke blew into my face. I coughed it out and moved through the people waiting for another bus and cut up a small alleyway. It emptied out to a bricked over pedestrian street with retail shop fronts and low budget street performers. The sun was out, so the people were too. I ploughed through the shoppers and tourists until I reached the top of the street. The crowds thinned out and I felt able to breathe for the first time in an hour. I crossed the street and entered a large park. It was a green area nestled in the middle of the city. On nice days it was packed with people strolling through or office workers sitting on the grass and the benches eating lunch. At night the park was closed and locked, so mainly it was the homeless and the drug addicts that stuck around after dark. I took a seat on a bench in front of a fountain. I listened to the

sounds of the green. Birds chirped, light wind rustled leaves, people chatted and that was all good. It was relaxing, that is until I started focusing on the sound of the fountain behind me. The water's steady stream made me have to piss so bad I could taste it. I took the pen from my pocket and pulled out a folded notebook. It was blank, but looked used. It was one that I carried around everywhere, normally in my inside breast pocket in case inspiration struck and I got the sense to write something down. Like I said, it was blank and probably had been for a year. I tried not to think about piss and flicked through the blank pages and imagined as I flipped each page with my thumb that well-handed script would appear on the sheets. It was the news story of the century captured first hand. Or maybe it was that novel I dreamed would come to me like magic one night, like Santa Clause or the Easter Bunny, I'd wake up with a hundred thousand words of pure literary genius out of nowhere. Who was I kidding? I was more likely to shit the bed or wake up magically with an STD. I sat there and waited for my mystery date. Five minutes past, then fifteen, then an hour. I still sat there. I still had to piss, but I'd manage to block out the flowing water sound through my miserable self loathing. Closing in

on two hours and I still sat on the bench. I had written my name in different fonts and sizes on several pages in my notebook, starting from the back and working in. I looked up and noticed the foot traffic through the park had fizzled out. Those walking in suits were no longer strolling, they were hustling. Those that remained were drug addicts, the zombies walking dead, and the hipsters with big shades, beards and flannels. And flip flops, don't forget flip flops. Hipsters wouldn't be hipsters if they couldn't expose their gross feet to the world non-stop.

My eyes bounced back and forth from the two types of patrons for a while. I found the two side by side odd but familiar. That had become Blackpool in a nutshell. Big Dick was right, the young rich set up shop next to the middle-age poor, one group hoping to offset the other, creating a balanced society so to speak. A girl caught my eye half a football field away and moving in my direction. Every few feet she would take a knee, put a camera in front of her that was bigger than her head and snap a few photos. I noticed her before, but didn't think much of it until she got closer. She walked in a weave side to side, not like she was drunk, more like she was feeling around for the right lighting. Despite her changing angles, the camera always pointed in the same direction. It was pointing towards me. Not like in my general vicinity or coincidently in the same direction, it was pointed at me specifically. I leaned my elbows onto my knees and looked closer. She walked across the green, zig zagging, then taking a knee, pointing and shooting. She was fifteen feet away before she stopped and let the camera hang loose from her neck. It looked to weigh as much as her. Her sunglasses hid most of her face and her hair was pulled back tightly. I spotted the curly frizz poking out from the back though and recognized her about the same time she stopped walking and her slim shadow shaded me from the sun.

'I know you.' I said. I was confused. It was all that came to me.

'No shit. You met me about twelve hours ago.'

'Probably closer to eighteen.' I said.

She pulled the camera up to her face again and snapped a photo an inch away from my nose. I blinked, I know I did. I always blink in pictures. She lifted the camera over her head, sat down and placed it on her lap.

'Can I see that notebook?' She asked.

I looked at it long and hard before handing it

over. She put the camera on the bench, took the notebook and stood up with it. She walked around the bench and threw the notebook into the water fountain behind us. Then she sat back down next to me. I looked at her. I didn't know what to say. Dumbfounded, I just sat there. I think I shrugged. I don't remember really, but I like to think I gave her that 'what the fuck' kind of open-palmed shrug.

She didn't acknowledge that she had just taken a part of my soul, my hopes and dreams and drowned them in a fountain. She reached into a slim bag that hung around her back and pulled out a thin laptop. She handed it over to me. I took it and moved it around in my hands.

'You've seen a laptop before I take it?' She asked.

'I've seen plenty of laptops sure. Just not sure what you're giving me this one for.'

'What did Big Dick say to you?'

'He told me where to go and said something along the lines of if you want to report the news, better start by being out there when it happens.'

'That's not what he said.'

'It was something along those lines, I don't remember exactly.'

She rolled her eyes, took the laptop, opened it

and pressed the on button. She handed it back to me then said, 'He said if you want to get readers, you have to be where the news happens and be the first to report it. Be the source he said. It's what he always says. He's a walking playlist of catch phrases.'

'Okay, yeah. That sounds familiar. So I've been out here now for two hours.'

'And you'll wait another two or ten or twelve or twenty four until something breaks.'

'Forgive me here, but who the hell are you in all this?'

'What do you mean?'

'What do I mean? You show up here, running the west coast weave with a camera in your hands and sunglasses bigger than two tinted fishbowls on strings.'

'Yeah, so?'

'Ugh.' I thought. This girl drove me crazy from the outset. 'Why were you taking pictures of me?'

'Who said I was?'

'Nobody said anything. I saw you.'

'Lotta things to take snaps of here, why'd you think I'd focus on you?'

'Yeah, that's my point.'

She smiled. She had nice dimples that I could

barely make out under those huge glasses and she had a gap between her front teeth that I found incredibly erotic. 'Maybe I think you're handsome, huh?'

I shook my head in agony. 'Yeah whatever.' I said. 'Listen. Big Dick's obviously paying you. Is it for photos. Are you the photographer?'

'Big Dick isn't paying me.'

'Then what . . . I don't even want to know.'

'You think I got something going on with Big Dick?'

The thought was enough to make me vomit on command. I choked it back.

She shook her head. I sensed disgust. That made me feel a little better. 'I'm an investor . . . and yeah, a photographer. A hobbyist at least.'

'You're investing? In what?'

She shook her head again and held her palms up. Her version of the 'what the fuck guy?'

'In you, you dumb shit. I know my way around this city and around a camera. I know websites, blah blah blah.' She said. Well not really blah blah blah, but it sounded like it to me.

'Okay then.' I said. 'You're an investor and a photographer and a whatever else. What, you just have spare dough lying around, approach Big Dick about it?'

'Not exactly. Big Dick came to me.'

'Why?'

'Big Dick's broke. Sorry to put it to you. He came to me for some start up cash.'

'Broke? Where the hell did his money go?'

She shrugged. 'Probably to me. How do you think I managed to save up? The Harlot's Den isn't exactly main street.' She must've saw the look on my face and assumed the hamster in my head was chugging on the wheel again. 'Listen Little Dick . . . ' She said.

'Ricky.' I said. Damn it.

'Listen Ricky, let me clear the air once and for all. I am not a stripper, or a prostitute, or someone that sleeps with old, fat, obnoxious drunk men.'

I stood there giving her reassuring nods trying to appear nonchalant, though inside I was quite excited she clarified her sexual status for me. I was beginning to get notions about our own potential for a little bit of foul play.

'Or their sons.' She said. 'So, can you get past it please?'

My internal joy died a quick death. 'Done.' I

said.

A looked away from her and gave the dwindling park another scan. As I did, a waft of something that reeked of sour milk climbed up my nostrils. The smell made me beg for sinusitis. I looked over at her and saw the owner of the awful scent appear behind her about the same moment I realized I didn't have a clue what this girl's name was. Otherwise, I would have yelled it out. I jumped up and said 'Hey!' in my best baritone. The girl turned her head quickly to look at the man who had crept up behind her.

'What the fuck?' She said. It sounded like she said it to me, but I guessed she'd just meant it generally.

The walking rotted corpse behind her smiled. The teeth he had left where black and yellow and looked like they got put through a pencil sharpener. 'Ain't that a nice camera honey?' He said. 'Let me get a look.'

'We don't want any trouble.' I said. He ignored me. She did too.

'The camera's mine. It is nice, I saved up a long time to buy it.'

'I bet you did.' The man said. He slowly reached his hand out for it. She pulled it toward her stomach, away from his reach. She turned to me and quickly shoved it into my free hand. I had the laptop folded under the other arm.

'Go for the camera again, you're gonna lose a hand.' She said. My jaw dropped with nerves and surprise. I hadn't considered that this strange girl would likely get me killed within twenty-four hours of seeing her for the first time. The man smiled again. It managed to look more devious this time. With his mouth open my nostrils caught another whiff of him. The guy was rotting from the inside out and the smell of that process seemed to pour out of his orifice.

'You're a little too cute and flimsy to make threats like that bitch.' The man said.

I thought for a moment I should appear indignant at his insult to a lady in my presence, but my balls were in my mouth with fear. Physical confrontations never really played to my strengths. I nearly swallowed my tongue as I watched him reach his hand over again slowly for the camera. I heard a sharp ringing noise, the sound of steel on steel. Her hand produced a long blade from nowhere and she held it to the man's throat, the point looked to be dug into his leathery neck skin.

'On second thought, I'll take your head off, not

your hand.' She said.

'It is the only way to kill a snake.' I thought. The man hesitated briefly then slowly backed away. He retreated to the shadows without another word. When he was out of sight, I walked over to some bushes and took a piss. With the heightened state of affairs, I'm not sure how I managed to keep the full bladder locked. I finished, gave my namesake a shake and walked back over to my unlikely hero. She was sitting on the bench observing the hipsters smiling through their beards, each with a plaid elbow in the grass. I found her casual nonchalance unsettling, but I didn't bring it up. It was obvious to me at that point that my new friend was an unpredictable lunatic. The thought of us together still aroused me, but my newfound fear of her existence would have surely made my unit chronically flaccid in her presence. 'What's your name?' I asked her when I sat back down.

'Veronica.' She said. She held her tiny hand over and I shook it. As I expected it was smooth and ice cold.

'They call you anything else, you know, for short?'

'Short for Veronica?'

'Yeah, like Ronnie or something like that?'

'I'm named after my grandmother, not a fucking moustache.'

I nodded my head. 'Understood.' After a minute of slowing my breathing it dawned on me that I'd had enough for the day, so I said as much. It went something like, 'So do you think we should call it . . . you know, after that guy and everything.'

She shook her head. 'Open up your laptop and be ready to type.'

'Be ready to type? Why?'

She pointed over towards the field of plaid. I followed the imaginary frozen rope her extended finger made until I saw our new friend emerge from the bushes behind the bearded assholes.

'It's about to go down.' She said. Next she took out her camera and started snapping photographs. I turned and watched her, half amazed, half confused until I heard a commotion. I opened up the laptop like she said. I couldn't make out what was being said, but the patch of grass had cleared out except for a few remaining tartans. Our emaciated friend grew animated, more so with every passing second.

'Here it comes.' I heard Veronica say. I didn't know if she was talking to me or herself. Her gaze stayed forward and she continued snapping photos. I squinted to keep the scene in focus. My fingertips rested on the keys with the blank word document at the ready, though I was unsure of where to begin. Veronica seemed to read my mind. 'Just wait for it, then write it like it happens.'

I nodded and kept my attention on the wiry dope head.

I watched a large hipster get up from the ground. He was the Bunyan of the group, bigger than you'd expect a man in tight plaid and skinny jeans to be. He stepped up to the bag of bones and put a hand to his chest. It didn't appear to be a shove from where I was standing, although the scrawny skeleton flew backwards like an empty Frito bag in the wind. He fell and rolled to the ground. Part of me was relieved thinking it was over until I saw him jump to his feet again and pull a knife from his pocket. He didn't bother going after the big one, he turned and stuck the knife into the closest flannel he could reach. That ended up being the chest of a kid that looked closer to fifteen than twenty five. He had a mop of blonde hair swooped to the side with a pound of pomade and sides shaved with a two blade. The indiscriminate violence stunned me. I had expected to see a small display of fisticuffs and record the witticisms of an irrational crack head in the park. The escalation to attempted murder really caught me on the back foot. I found myself standing up in scared outrage. I turned to Veronica with my mouth wide opened. She looked unsurprised. 'Keep watching.' She said.

'We should call the police . . . or ambulance, or do something.' I said.

She held the phone in her hand up for me to see. 'It's dialing.' She said. I watched her put the phone to her ear and being talking. Her coolness led me to be anything but. I was cold. I had goose bumps on my skin, but I was also sweating. Every so often a bead from my sweat moustache dropped down to my lips and I could taste my own fear. I sat back down in the knowledge there was little I could do for now, having no discernible skill in either physical combat or first aid. The young man with a knife in his chest looked as surprised at the escalation of violence as I had been. He was on the ground in shock. Most of his friends had formed a wall around him. An aerial view would've looked like a patchwork quilt. I scanned the grass for the perpetrator, the wacky unpredictable being that had instantly changed his persona from an unfortunate side effect of pharma-industry corruption and gentrification to a malignant tumor of society that

needs eradication at any cost. He'd undoubtedly run off. I followed the nervous gaze of the hipsters down the concrete path leading deeper into the park and listened for the hurried crack of track suit bottoms. I spotted the man in the distance. He walked quickly with a bouncy limp that must be a prerequisite for drug addicts everywhere. Every few steps he'd glance back towards the crowd, but he didn't stop walking. His clumsy getaway continued. The few pedestrians on the path gave him a wide birth. Sirens began to pollute the air. There were multiple sets of them that contrasted poorly like listening to Bob Seger when you're roommate had Snoop on in the living room. I looked back over to the group of young guys. Friends hovered now over the victim so that I couldn't see him. I was sad and panicked. I looked over at Veronica. She was off the phone and taking pictures frantically. She at least had the decency to leave the flash off. Our collective aim was to be among the news, to capture it first. I didn't expect we'd have any success from the outset. I guess I should have felt good in a way at the progress. Instead I felt cheap and voyeuristic. I felt like I violated some ancient pact with my city, one that said its underbelly could be discussed verbally in suburban kitchens over wine

and pizza, but not documented for literary consumption.

As the first responders trickled into the park with navy blue uniforms and bright orange bags I immediately began to feel better. I watched the patchwork quilt slowly unravel to let the professionals get to work. I lifted my laptop and began to type. I set the scene quickly and gave the facts in as much gruesome glory as possible without obvious hyperbole. Only then did my words begin to meander over opinion and conjecture. I was on fire, running on fumes of adrenaline. The crackle of the keys as I frantically typed was music to my ears that I never wanted to cease. Then a loud pop echoed through the green. My musical typing stopped. I looked around. No one else appeared to notice the sound. I stood up with the laptop in my hands. I looked down the concrete path that our subject used as a getaway. It was near empty. The exception was a track suited bag of bones at rest in a pool of red blood. I was too far away at the time to see it clearly, but I would later describe the hole between his eyebrows as a sideways kiss of thick red lipsticked lips.

3

Let me explain one or two things about hipsters and day jobs before we go any further. I don't hate hipsters. Hate is such a strong word. It's a strong emotion that just gets tossed around with too much ease, much like its antonym. Neither word should be used lightly but both are. Really think about it. There're plenty of things you probably dislike or would rather do without, but those things you truly hate should hopefully be few. It's a word that should only rear its ugly head for things like child molesters, Hitler, and rental car companies. Honestly just one time, give me the car I booked for the price I agreed to pay for it. Just once, please, for the love of Christ. Sorry, anyway, I was saying I don't hate hipsters. I find them laughable and pretentious. They're rich kids acting poor and they genuinely believe they are the counter culture. It's a cliché at its most douchey.

Face it, if you're emotionally dependent on any corporation, i.e. live inside your smartphone and post pictures of your bearded mug and the shit you ate on Facebook and Twitter every ten seconds, then you are most certainly not counter culture. You're on the corporate bandwagon with everyone else. Recognize it and move on.

Yeah, okay, they're irritating, but they're also harmless. They probably even do some good for society. I like craft beer and quirky eateries as much as any of those douche bags. It's all upside for me.

That leads me to my day job. Growing up I always wanted to follow in Big Dick's footsteps. I'm not his biggest fan now, but a boy grows up wanting to emulate his dad, at least for a while. For me, it was a long while. Honestly, I still want the same. Big Dick wasn't exactly a beacon of wisdom, but one thing he said that stuck with me is that if I really wanted to write then by all means don't ever pick up another skill. Don't learn a trade or go to law school or any of that. He said as soon as you have something to fall back on you will do just that because every writer fails. Every writer is a failure until that day when you wake up and realize that writing is your only job. That means no waiting tables, serving coffee, putting vinyl siding on houses, nothing. You wake up, you kick around whether you'll shower or not, you'll sit for a few hours and hammer on those keys. Regardless of sales or popularity, it's at that point the writer is no longer a failure. So in true hackneyed fashion I ignored the one bit of worthwhile unsolicited advice from my old man and went to college for business. Long story short, if that's still possible, I go to an office and wear khakis or a suit with gingham shirts and French cuffs that rattle on my laminated desk as I type memos or move my mouse around every few minutes to stop my computer from locking me out due to non-use while I day dream or stare at the clock. Now as I told you already, there was a period of time when I was purely trying to make it freelancing. When the shit hit the fan with my faux starlet story, my back was against the wall. So it was sleep on the street or get my old job back. I'd left abruptly over a year ago, but it wasn't on bad terms. People in companies hire who they know. It's easier than spinning your wheels interviewing a hundred carbon copies of the same person and you know what you're getting.

So I got my old job back. It took about thirty minutes in the office to remember exactly why I left

the last time. The stories at lunch were the same. The day to day bullshit was the same. Everyone was still convinced they're busier and more stressed than anyone else and they seemed to need this in order to validate their self-worth. The same brand of eager beavers were running around like they're having an impact on something huge, something life changing, while really it just hasn't dawned on them that nothing they do matters at all anywhere in the world and it never will. There was still the same people that came in early and stayed late and spent the majority of their time during the day telling everyone what time they got in that morning and what time they left last night while producing no discernible results. The people paid to look after the employees' wellbeing and company's culture were still dicks. The guys in finance couldn't see past their spreadsheets and the guys in operations couldn't talk to each other without fifty Power Point slides to point at while doing it. I won't even elaborate on the email tough guys. Worst of all, I still didn't get it. I did everything every teacher, guidance counselor, aunt, uncle and neighbor told me was the thing I had to do, the thing that was the envy of all, that would get me to the end game. What is that you ask? Apparently it's a fucking

middle management white collar job where a handful of white men make a shit-ton of cash while everyone else buries themselves in student debt, finance cars they only drive to and from the office in, bend over and take a stiff one from the bank for a house they pretty much only sleep in and then work their balls off to pay it all off just in time to die. So, needless to say I was glad to back.

After I wrote my article, I handed it off to Veronica then excused myself. I needed to think or so I believed until I got home and was alone with my thoughts. I kept reliving the same scene in my head, a pool of plaid blood on the ground surrounded by shocked and outraged faces. I couldn't sleep. I was haunted. I poured some cheap wine into a pint glass and drank it quickly. Then I smoked a handful of cigarillos one after another while drinking a coffee mug filled with whiskey and boiled water. It was enough eventually to knock me out. I woke up thirsty as hell and extremely groggy.

I arrived at my desk that morning surely stinking of whiskey and vanilla cigars. I opened a spreadsheet, a Word document, a desktop folder and a soft core smut website. I alt-tabbed back and forth for a couple of hours, timing the rotation to the coming and going

of my boss Larry, who was five years my junior and formerly my assistant in the accounts department. He wasn't a bad guy, I didn't mind him most of the time. There was a week or two after he read the Steve Jobs biography where he walked around in a turtle neck and gave out shit to everyone, but that seemed to level set after a while. I watched him walk past me with a notebook and folded laptop under his arm. He smiled with no teeth and gave me a slight head nod. When I heard the door behind me shut I flicked back to the Russian blonde in a crop top I was beginning to analyze. I heard a throat clear behind me and I nearly jumped. It was too slow, but I hit the lock screen buttons to draw less attention to my creepiness. I looked up and gave my most disarming smile and hello I could muster. The secretary for our floor stood over me. She was a nice motherly woman in her late fifties. I could tell she was embarrassed. I couldn't tell if it was of me or for me.

'Sorry to disturb you.' She said.

I responded with something like, 'Oh no, no problem. blah blah blah, I'm not really a pervert.'

'There's someone downstairs to see you.' She said.

'Really? Hmm.' I said.

'She didn't give a name. Told reception you would be expecting her.'

'Her?'

'So I'm told. You want me to get more information? Tell her you're . . . busy?'

'No, no.' I said, standing up and putting on my suit coat. 'I just uh, I forgot she was coming in. I'll head down there. Thanks.'

She said nothing else. She didn't smile or wave good bye either, just meekly headed back to her desk.

'It's settled.' I thought. 'I've been judged.' I pushed through the door to the hall and took the elevator down to the ground floor. It was slow moving and I was impatient. Plus I was nervous because whoever was next to get into the elevator was sure to inhale my boozy stench and if they saw me, I would likely be judged once again and I was still getting over the last couple of minutes. The elevator finally stopped at the bottom floor. I stepped out quickly and walked down the hall. I was conscious of the floor squeaking under my cheap rubber soles. I tried to walk lighter and higher on my toes to limit the sound effects. I reached reception and glanced around the waiting area. I saw a girl in high shoes and slim socks pulled to her upper calf. Her legs were crossed one over the other. I watched the top one bounce rhythmically for a few seconds. Her skirt was short, very short. I hadn't noticed how long her legs were previously or how her thighs thickened as they meandered to her . . . waist. I swallowed my saliva and walked through the twist barrier. She heard the squeak of my shoes and looked up at me over the coffee table magazine she held in her hands.

'Veronica.' I said. A more confident man would have probably led with 'Hello' or 'Hi'. Instead I greeted her with her own name and nearly phrased the word itself in the tone of a question.

'Little Dicky.' She said. She dropped the magazine to the table and uncrossed her legs.

I admit. I was transfixed. I would've like to have had the opportunity again, to at least pretend to look away as opposed to foaming at the mouth because I managed a glimpse of her black laced underwear, if you could call it that.

She stood up and said 'let's take a walk.' I nodded. I followed her out the door. The woman behind the reception desk smirked at me. I could feel my ears burning and knew my cheeks were crimson. Veronica walked in front of me. I followed the subtle bounce of her hips until she reached the cross walk

and stopped. She smiled at me finally and I smiled back. I started to settle down and we walked across the street side by side when the green man signal beeped.

'I didn't expect you to drop into my office.' I said.

'Why not?'

'Why didn't I expect you?'

'Yeah. Seems like a reasonable thing to stop by someone's work to go for coffee or lunch.'

'Is that what we're doing?' I asked. She shrugged. Across the street was a tree lined plaza. We took a seat on a slab of granite. My hands burned as I leaned on the rock to sit down. I wondered if her upper thighs felt the sting as well when she sat down. Obviously I didn't ask her and she didn't voluntarily share anything of such an intimate nature.

'I'm not hungry.' She said. 'Let's sit here for a minute.'

'No problem.' I said. 'I've got plenty of time.'

'How long do you get for lunch?'

'I don't get anything specific. I just kind of take it. I'm usually alone, so I don't take long.'

'You don't need to work now, you know. Big Dick and I have a few things going now. I'm sure we

can set aside cash to keep you afloat. It would keep you focused on what we're doing.'

I shrugged. 'I'm okay for now.'

'You think you can do both? Put out a good product for us and work full time?'

'I'll figure it out. I'm just pulling myself back after a pretty dry stretch. Let's just say I can't put all my eggs in Big Dick's basket.'

She laughed a little. That made me feel good for a change. 'I bet that didn't come out the way you meant it.'

'It never usually does.' I said. She smiled again and I smiled back. I found her flash of humility comforting and began to relax.

'Listen, if push comes to shove, I can prioritize the journalism over anything else.'

'Won't that jam you up here? If it means not showing up or at least not mentally showing up?'

'I highly doubt it. Anyone that matters in there doesn't have a clue who I am and anyone that minds won't have the balls to call me out on something. Confrontation doesn't fly in these types of offices. Passive aggression yes, but outright confrontation, never. I might as well keep showing up while they continue to pay me.'

'Okay.' She said. 'Suit yourself.' She reached into her slim bag, the strap of which pulled tightly down the center of her chest accentuating her perkiness. She pulled out a small stack of papers and handed them to me. I took them and leafed through the top few. There were random stains on the printouts that looked like the rim of a wet glass and several dried spills. The text was typewritten with a whole lot of red marks crossing out lines and sloppy handwriting in the margins.

'Big Dick sends his notes on your article.' She said.

'I see that.' I leafed through a few more pages, it was more of the same. I held the stack closer to my nose. I could actually whiff the old man's scent off the pages. 'Wait, I thought we ran the article immediately?'

She nodded her head. 'We did. It's up there and it's getting views, a lot of them. I've used more photos this time to try and . . . well, you know, mask some of the articles lesser elements.'

I was angry. The anger was offset by my growing infatuation as much as the fact that I was still scared of the girl after the whole threatening to decapitate a dangerous hobo incident.

'So he wants me to put through some updates.'

'Yeah, asap. That's the beauty of running this thing digital only, real time updates.'

'I guess.'

'I see you're angry.' She said. 'Don't be. Big Dick's just trying to help. I know he's an old drunken slob, but from what I've heard and read, he had his day and he knows what he's talking about when it comes to this stuff.'

I knew she was right. It didn't make it any better. I looked at the papers again and chuckled.

'What?' She asked.

'His handwriting . . . it hasn't changed. Reminds me of when I was a kid.'

'He write you many notes? Filled with fatherly advice no doubt.'

'He used to get me to practice forging his signature and mimic his handwriting.'

'Why the hell would he do that?'

I laughed at the thought. 'So I wouldn't bother him with shit like field trip permission slips and responding to requests for meetings from teachers and things like that.'

She smiled but didn't say anything. She appeared to absorb the comment and chew it up to get the flavor. I was just glad we were having a real conversation.

'Is there a short version of what he wants changed?' I asked.

'For one, use smaller words. If you're using a three-syllable word when a one or two-syllable word will do, then you're just being a cunt.'

'Uh . . .okay.'

'And lose the adverbs. We're not writing a literary novel here, we're reporting the news. It needs to be quick, clear and punchy. We're competing with click bait headlines and bullet point lists, top five things to know this morning, the six at six, the eight at eight. You get the point. Our audience is fickle with strobe light attention span. If your describing blood as crimson or magenta instead of just red, we're gonna have a problem.'

'Jesus Christ. Your point is made.'

'Okay. Good.'

'Anything else?'

'Yes. You wrote one story instead of two.'

'What two?'

'We have a badly injured college kid in the hospital and we have a dead white male in the park. You link one with the other and you have a headline that says drug addict attacks gang member in park, one dead, one injured. Case open and shut. Joe Schmo reads that, drugs are bad, gangs are bad, no fucking shit, no news there, I'm safe watching TV in the suburbs. Whereas, you should have one seriously injured young man, stabbed while minding his own business in the park during the day. Meanwhile on the same day in that very same park there's a random attack on a middle age man, potentially a jogger as inferred from his track attire and slim build, blah blah blah. Then all of a sudden you have violence that's local, random and unsolved. Suddenly Joe Schmo isn't so comfortable anymore. He's double checking his doors are locked and he's looking over his shoulder on his walk to the train. What's more is, he's keeping an eye on the news to see if anything else develops.'

'Okay.' I said. 'I think I get what you're saying. Keep them scared and you keep them hooked.'

'Pretty much. The bottom line is, if we want people to keep coming back to our site, which we do, then when it comes to reporting on violence, the preference is to paint it as local, random and unsolved. Just like I said. At least for now that is. Big Dick knows what demographic he's looking for today. That's all subject to change at any stage. But today, that's the approach.'

'Even if . . . you know, it's not true?'

'You're reporting facts, based on what you've seen. You don't know what's true and what's not. You don't know motives. Did you see who stabbed who? The actual act of penetration, did you see it?'

I thought about it for a few seconds before responding. 'No. I guess I didn't see it start to finish, but. . .'

'And you heard a shot from someplace sure. But did you get up close and identify the man on the ground, lying in his pool of blood. Did you see who it was? Did you see who pulled the trigger, if that's indeed what happened?'

'I . . . I did not.'

'You're not making anything up.'

'Maybe not, but I'm not reporting the truth either.'

'You ever heard of reader's inference?'

'Yeah sure, I know what it is. I've been on the losing end of reader's inference in a big way.'

'That's right. Sorry.'

'Don't worry about it.'

'We're not asking you to defame anyone or anything. Actually, it's best you don't for now. We just

need you to produce the facts, but do so in a way that you leave the door open for interpretation.'

I thought about this for a minute or two before responding. I wasn't comfortable with what she wanted me to do. That said, I wasn't really comfortable with any of it. It was all too murky. Big Dick's motive, Veronica's stake in the success of this . . . whatever it was we were doing. Was my foolish desire to be a slick-haired, sport jacket and cravat wearing master of the pen so powerful as to blind me from logical thought all together? Short answer is yes, obviously, or else I wouldn't have led you to believe otherwise. I gathered the strength to ask one question at least.

'Let me ask you one thing at least?'

'Go for it.'

'That park. How did Big Dick know something would go down in that park? He could've sent me anywhere in the whole city, but he didn't. He sent me to that spot. I checked this morning, there were no other shootings, stabbings, murders or otherwise noteworthy crimes in the city yesterday. Well, at least none that made any headlines as of yet. It all seems a little too . . . fortuitous, if you ask me.'

'Could've just said lucky. That's exactly the point

I'm trying to make.'

'Yeah, right, okay, so it was so lucky. Well, lucky for us I guess, not so much some other guys.'

'He didn't send you there.'

'Oh no?'

'I did.'

A sinking feeling quickly came to my stomach. I looked at her with what I imagine was a furrowed brow.

'Relax Little Dick.' She said.

'Ricky. Please.'

'Ricky, relax. You've heard of big data? *Moneyball*?'

'Sure. I've heard of it.'

'It works for crime statistics too.'

'Okay, so what? You got your hands on some data, ran some pivot tables and voilà?'

'No.'

'More than that?'

'Much more.'

'Okay, whatever you did, you picked a place in the city more than likely to see some violence on a mid-summer's eve?'

'Yes.'

'Wait, but if that's out there, wouldn't . . . you

know the cops be working on the same set of assumptions.'

'If they had the capability, I'm sure they would.'

'Wouldn't it make sense to, I don't know, keep them in loop or something. Seems like it might . . . '

'Out of the question.'

'Yeah, but, you want to elaborate?'

'Not at all.' She reached into her bag again and pulled out a small card. I took it. It looked like a standard business card, but it just had an address on it. 'You know the address?'

'Harlot's Den?'

'Close, it's upstairs. Doorway to the left of the bar entrance. Come after work.' She stood up and adjusted the bag, pulling it tightly down the middle of her chest. She looked me up and down as she did it. 'Get changed first. Something darker, less douchey.' I looked down at my clothes. I wasn't exactly on the cover of GQ, but I thought it was a harsh criticism. 'We're done here.' She said. She turned abruptly and headed off down the street. I watched her walk away gripping the card she handed me tightly between my thumb and index finger. I kept my eyes on the slit of her skirt like the creep that I had suddenly morphed into until she finally disappeared around the corner.

'She lives at the Harlot's Den.' I said to myself. 'Of course she does.'

4

I hadn't turned on the television in my apartment for at least a month. I could be exaggerating slightly, but not by much. I used the screen more frequently as a mirror than anything else. I was considering moving my furniture around to point it at some other arbitrary object in the small sitting room, something less reflective so I didn't have to keep staring at myself every time I sat on the couch. If only I had a fire place. After talking with Veronica I went back into work for a little while, but I couldn't sit there for long. My mind had wandered far elsewhere and couldn't settle back into that mundanity. Her high socks and bare thighs were imprinted deep into my psyche and it made it impossible to hold up a front of pretending to work. So I left the office and went home. I'm not sure if anyone cared, I didn't bother asking. I got home and went straight to my closet to find

something "less douchey". It was more difficult than I expected, but I eventually landed on navy blue jeans and a charcoal grey hoody. She said dark, so I did my best. It was then that I realized, for a pretty morose guy, I owned a lot of pastels. I gave myself a spritz of cologne and checked my reflection in the blank television screen on my way out.

By the time I reached the turn for Harlot's lane (not the actual street name, but it fits, so I'm sticking with it), I was wishing I'd dipped a t-shirt in that cologne and brought it with me to huff as I made my way down that street. I nearly considered doing so with one of my socks instead of breathing in the piss and vomit that perfumed the environment. I was early, so I walked past Veronica's door and walked into the bar to see if the old man was around. It was darker inside than out. The music and lighting was more subdued than my last visit, but the stench of the place seemed more poignant partially because it hadn't yet been masked by cigarette smoke. There was a man behind the bar instead of Veronica. He was muscular with a square jaw and a smooth bald head. It was an impressive wax job, one to put Lex Luthor red with jealous rage. I walked up to the bar. He smiled and said hello.

'Hey.' I said.

'Get you a drink?' He asked.

'What beers you have in a bottle?' He looked at me like he bit into onion. I didn't care, I'd learned my lesson. Fool me twice and all that. He reached into a short refrigerator behind the bar under the cash register. He wrapped each finger around a bottle top and pulled them out for me to see. I pointed at the only green bottle. It had a label I didn't recognize but it could only be an improvement. He put the others down and popped the top off the bottle. His arms flexed with the motion and I thought his sleeves nearly tore off. 'Fucking hero.' I thought, obviously feeling jealous and just a little pathetic in his presence.

'You seen Dick Sherman today?' I asked.

'Big Dick?'

Jesus Christ. 'Yeah, that's the one.'

'Around back.'

'Thanks.' I said. I gave over the cash for the beer. I rounded the corner same as before and entered the back bar. It looked different in the daylight, if you could call it that. It was empty. The music was on, but it was pure background only. I walked deeper into the room. The further I went, the darker the lighting

grew, though an intermittent strobe from a disco ball reflected light in random square shaped patterns on the back wall. I fought back the urge to mutter 'Dad.' It would've sounded desperate and really out of place in that establishment. There was a door opened slightly in the corner of the room that let out a pizza slice of light. I slowly walked towards it. A lump formed in my throat as I got closer. The further away from the music I went, the more I was able to make out grunting and soft moaning noises coming from the room. When I was only a few feet away, I could hear beyond those sounds to the slapping of skin and thumping of bones and muscles. I grew aroused from instinct, but seconds later a sick feeling was rising in my gut. I was too close to back away by the time I pieced together what the noises meant. My eyes focused on a slim and taut female back. She had messy black hair bouncing over her back and shoulders in a rhythm consistent with the slapping noises. I was just glad to see it wasn't the fuzzy brown of Veronica's hair color.

'Junior, what the fuck?' I heard a voice say from behind me. I turned, relieved to see Big Dick walking towards me, the men's room door swinging behind him.

'Dad . . . sorry, I thought . . .'

'Come on Little Dick, the guy came here to get fucked in peace, not in front of an audience. He doesn't need your eyes on his uglies.'

'I wasn't looking at his uglies.'

'I fucking hope not.' He walked over and took a seat at the bar. He sat in front of a whiskey glass and a half empty pint. Both of which I should've noticed when I walked in. I took a long drink from my beer and put it on the bar. I skipped a stool and took one two spots away from him.

'You want something else?' He asked. I waved him off.

'I'm here on assignment, not staying long.' I pointed upstairs. 'I'm here to meet Veronica.'

'Good.' He said. 'She give you my notes?'

'She did.'

'Good. I trust there're no questions.' He said without bothering to look at me.

I took it as a statement instead of a question. I felt instantly awkward and disappointed.

'You could just call me next time. Or, better yet, I could come in and talk to you about your pointers.'

'We'll keep working through Ronny.' He said. I fucking knew she went by Ronny, tried to fob me off on a moustache joke.

'I need to keep distance.' Big Dick said.

I knew what he meant. It was always the same with him. Regardless, I asked 'Distance huh? From me or the work?'

He didn't say anything right away. He drank the rest of his beer. So did I. Then he just said, 'Separate houses.' He said it more to himself than to me. It was true sure, but it was also an excuse. There was no use having it out about thirty plus years of neglect right then. Plus it would've come across as champagne problems in that den of sin.

I just said, 'Sure.' I slid my empty beer closer to the edge of the bar. I stood up and turned to walk out. I didn't bother with a goodbye.

'Hey.' He called. I stopped and turned my head. 'Tell Ronny to see me when she's done tonight.'

I stayed silent again, just paused for a moment and then kept walking out. In the front bar, the bartender said something to me in passing. I ignored him and his biceps. I couldn't breathe in that shithole any longer. Out front I took in a deep breath forgetting about the incessant stench of urine. The deep breath was like taking a bite out of that foul air. I blew it out quickly. I turned to the door next to the

Harlot's Den entrance. I couldn't see a bell to ring. I went to knock, but the door pushed open slightly when I did. I walked in and shut it behind me. A single light bulb hung from a wire in the ceiling inside the hallway. Its dim glare lit just barely to the top of the steep staircase leading to Veronica's apartment door. I climbed the steps and stood on the landing for a few seconds. I paused to listen to muffled voices from inside the apartment. After a few more seconds, I knocked on her door. It opened abruptly almost before I took my hand away. I stood face to face with one tall well-dressed gentleman with dark hair, sallow skin and designer stubble. An equally dapper black guy stood behind him. The man in front smiled at me and said hello. Caught off guard, I just glared at them both. Veronica slid past the men in the doorway and looked out at me. 'You're early.' She said. I just shrugged. The handsome devil in front of me said something like 'Well, I'll leave you to it.' He leaned over and kissed Veronica. It was on the cheek, but I think there was some side lip action. The guy behind him did the same and at the same time slid something into the back pocket of her jeans. It looked like a small envelope. I was appalled and jealous, particularly by the proximity of the man's

hand to her ass. Keep in mind, I had absolutely no rational basis for either emotion. Nonetheless they were there. In response, I squared my shoulders so both men had to shift their own sideways to slide past me. I thought I saw Veronica roll her eyes at me, but I couldn't be certain. Both men said goodbye to her and to me as they slipped by me so close I could smell them. Also, I have to say, genuinely, I've never encountered a pair of men that smelled so delicious. Had I not taken the immediate decision to be a cock towards them, I would've been hounding each for their brand of deodorant and daily skin routine. They were down the stairs and out the door in seconds, at which time I stood alone on the landing, confused and looking like an absolute bollocks. Veronica had already turned to walk away.

I stepped into the narrow corridor of her apartment. 'Close the door behind you.' She said as she walked away. I did as instructed and slowly followed her down the hall. The entrance was in need of a paint job and the walls were bare except for a small plaque that looked like a crucifix with a prayer attached hung over the doorway to the kitchen. I followed her in quickly, so I didn't take time to read what it said. She walked into a room off of the

kitchen. It looked like a bedroom so I didn't follow her. I put my hand on one of the chairs pushed into the small table. It must have scraped off the ground because she yelled from the room 'Don't bother sitting, we're leaving.'

I took my hand off of the chair and stood there holding my wrist awkwardly with my other hand. She poked her head back into the kitchen, looked at my odd posture and squinted. 'Come on.' She said. 'We're going, follow me.'

I walked into the room behind her. I was right, it was her bedroom. I didn't have time for a full perv out session of its contents, but what struck me at once was the daintiness of it. I don't know what I would have expected, black satin sheets, whips, chains, a crossbow over the headboard maybe. It had none of that. The room was tidy, bright and had white and lavender bed sheets and matching curtains. She opened the curtains fully and opened up a window. It let out onto a fire escape landing. She waved me along and I followed her out. She shut the window tightly and set something in the sash. When she stood up straight, we were face to face. The landing was tight and forced us very close together. 'It's good to know whether someone has climbed through before me.'

She said. I just nodded. We were close enough that I could smell her lip gloss. It was a cherry and mint concoction. I was lightheaded with euphoria. Then she said 'can you get the fuck out of my way?'

I slid to the side to let her get by me. She held onto my hips as she worked her way over. She kicked down a trap ladder and led the way down. At the bottom there was a drop. She landed like an agile feline. I landed like a dead elephant. She had me jump and shove the ladder back into place afterwards. It took two attempts, but I thought it went well enough and I showed off some upper body strength for a change. The back alley reeked much worse than the front. Instead of just urine, it was urine and garbage. I didn't see any rats at that moment, but I knew they were close. I followed her down the alley and around the corner to a small red Volkswagen. It was old. That's the best thing I can say about it. She got into the driver's seat and reached across to unlock the passenger door. I sat down into the seat and my knees were jammed between the dashboard and my chest. 'Cozy.' I said. I managed to reach underneath and pull a latch to buy me a few inches.

We drove off out of the alley way and into the city streets. It was dark by this time and the city lights

shone around us as we drove. She followed the river that ran through the city's heart for a couple of miles. I watched as the red, blue and yellow lights from the riverfront bars and clubs reflected off of the water. The colors bouncing off of the slow ripples gave the water a pulse. Over the radio static I asked, 'You gonna fill me in on where we're headed?'

She glanced over at me quickly. 'We're gonna stakeout a neighborhood and wait for something to happen.' My mind jumped right to opportunity first. I kicked myself for not bringing mints or gum. I thought about what she said a little more then. Another thought nipped at me.

'Wait, what neighborhood?' I asked. I grew nervous at the thought. Crazy or not this girl could not protect me in just any ole Blackpool neighborhood, and forget about me being able to watch after her. She must have smelled my fear. She turned and smiled at me.

'You'll see.' She said. It wasn't comforting. I began to follow her route more closely. I watched as streets past by my window that I preferred not to walk down. To my surprise, she turned onto the highway and headed away from the city. I was confused. I looked over at her as we changed lanes and picked up

speed. 'We heading to the burbs?' I asked.

'You ask a lot of fucking questions. Can't you just follow along on these things and not worry so much.'

I thought about it. 'Uh, no.' I said. 'Not anymore I can't. I think I've been left in the dark enough.' I felt her roll her eyes again. She didn't answer and to put an exclamation point on the topic, she turned the radio up despite the fact it sounded more like microwave popcorn than music.

Less than fifteen minutes later, she moved over a lane and took the exit. We followed a winding road for another minute and emptied out to a small town. I hadn't been there before, but it looked like your standard commuter town. I saw a sign for a train station. We drove past it and down what I guessed was main street as indicated by the location of a bank, a bar and a church. She pulled down a side street, then made another turn into a tree-lined neighborhood. She pulled up to the curb and parked the car nestled under one of the trees. I scratched my head and looked around the housing estate. The row of houses all looked the same, brick with white trim. Each house had at least two cars parked in the driveway. The street was beyond my price range and would be for some time. That much I knew for certain. 'We're looking for something to pop off around here? It doesn't make sense. It's too nice around here.' I said.

'It is too nice, that's just the point. If you were gonna knock a place off, would you rob the Queen's palace or the servant's quarters?'

'Huh?'

'Guys that rob houses don't hit Dewey's apartment that works down the corner store. Well, maybe they do, but that's just addicts. They'll rob their grandma's house if they have to. But if you're actually looking to make off with something decent without much hassle, here's where you want to be.'

'You seem to know a little bit about this.'

'It's called research Little Dicky. We left the city and drove four exits west off the highway. The three we past all have similar neighborhoods and there's been at least one home invasion in each in the last week.'

'So you think this place is next?'

'I'm betting my precious time on it aren't I?'

'Come on though. Look at all these places. There are lights on in almost every house. They all probably have alarms too.'

Veronica smiled at me and shook her head. She opened her door and got out of the car. I saw her duck behind the trees, but I could still see her shadow in the street courtesy of the street lights. I opened the door and stood halfway out of the car. 'Hey.' I said in a forceful whisper.

'I'll be right back.' She said. 'Get in the car and keep watching.'

I did as I was told. I saw her dark shape slip into someone's front yard, but lost sight of her shortly after. With the car off, the radio stopped. The neighborhood was dead silent. All I could hear was my own breathing and the blood thumping in my ears. Both rhythms picked up speed when I started to panic. A few seconds later a house alarm started shrieking nearby. I felt my heart pounding in my chest. Part of me wanted to jump in the driver's seat and take off. My head was spinning around like a bobbin-head doll on the dash of an off-roader. Less than a minute later I saw an elongated shadow moving in the street. I stretched my neck to look over and saw Veronica walking very calmly back towards the car. She opened the door and got in.

'What the fuck is wrong with you?' I asked.

'I'm proving a point. Watch. Don't worry the

alarms only go like that for five to ten minutes then they reset.'

We waited out the noise. I was waiting for a flood of neighbors to walk out their front doors and see what was afoot or to see a police cruiser pass by for a checkup. The alarm stopped after five minutes. There was nothing, no movement whatsoever, not even a curtain opening for a peak out the window. I was perplexed to say the least.

'Vacation season.' Veronica said. 'All it takes is a ball to hit off the door or a strong gust of wind and an alarm is set off while the owners are off getting sand in their crotches somewhere better than here. After a while, the neighbors just block it out.'

'The mid to upper middle class home crying wolf.' I said.

'I guess you could say that.' She reached into her bag and handed me over the laptop. 'It's clumsy though, come up with something better for the piece. You might as well set the scene while we wait.'

That's what I did, I wrote a piece, one that I thought was promising and eye opening. I highlighted the spate of burglaries in pleasant estates that happened to have easy access to the highway just like Veronica said. I also came up with a few analogies I thought were passable and stuck them in. Although I was later informed that they were self-indulgent and added nothing to the story. Subsequently, I was instructed to remove all attempts at intelligence and just make the points we were trying to make without the pathetic attempts at literary flair. The punchline for the story came shortly after I stopped typing the draft, about an hour in all after we parked.

Veronica put her hand gently on my forearm. Her touch made my arm tingle and it ran up my neck. I looked up at her and she pointed to our twelve o'clock. We're on she said. She pulled out her oversized camera and held it at the ready. I shifted in the passenger seat with the laptop hot and humming on my knees. I heard a van door shut in the distance and soon saw two men walking down the street. They did their best to walk steady and nonchalantly as they moved in the shadows under the line of trees. Because I was looking for it, I could tell they were doing some final casing of the houses they past. I followed their movements closely.

'Stay low.' Veronica said. 'They probably won't make it this far down.'

As soon as she said that I got really nervous. It

hadn't occurred to me that anyone out to take off one of the houses would notice us sitting and watching first hand. Within a few seconds it became clear that's exactly what was going to happened. I froze with fear, again. Veronica quickly jumped over the center console and before I knew it her legs straddled me and her tongue was down my throat. I felt her hips thrusting rhythmically against me and my namesake reacted accordingly. My hands went instinctively to her back and pulled her closer. I felt her hands up near my face and pulling at the back of my hair. My nerves melted away. 'This is it.' I thought. 'It wasn't just me, she felt it too.' Then, as abruptly as it had started, it ended. She pulled away and forcefully pushed my head back against the headrest. I stared wide-eyed at her in shock and confusion. 'Bollocks.' I thought.

'It's on.' She said. She climbed back over to the driver's seat, but stayed facing behind us. 'They just took off for that house on the corner. I think I saw one leap the side gate.' I hadn't moved yet. I wasn't quite ready. She looked at me and held her palms up at me. I turned and looked in the direction she pointed. 'They're going for the patio door in the back I bet.' She said. 'Put that down in your article too. Patio doors equal easy targets.'

'I haven't heard any alarm yet.'

She shook her head. 'No, you're right. They're in though, I know it. My guess is they cased the entire neighborhood today or over the course of the week. See what happens is that anyone with a dog or a monitored alarm gets noted. The standard system that just rings out and those houses with nothing, they get prioritized.'

'My douchebag boss would call that low hanging fruit.'

She looked over at me and smiled. I felt like finally, one landed with her. She pulled out her phone and dialed a number. 'I'm calling it in. Start timing now.' She said.

Seconds later she was on the line with the dispatcher. She hung on the line for close to five minutes. It was long enough to report to the dispatcher that the two men just pulled out of the driveway in the homeowners SUV. We both ducked down again as they past. They drove right out of the housing estate without a second thought. They must have had a third player involved because the van that dropped them off was gone too. When Veronica hung up, we stayed waiting. Another twenty minutes went by. She kept snapping photos, plus she had her camera phone recording now.

'We really need to stick around any longer?'

'We're waiting on the punchline.' She said.

'Which is?'

She smiled. 'Police response time.'

I shook my head. 'Remind me why we're here?'

'You mean like what's the meaning of life?'

'I mean like, what's this article trying to do?'

'Get suburbia uncomfortable in their own homes.'

'And that helps our cause?'

'If it gets us readers it helps the cause.'

'It seems cheap. Plus, I mean there's bigger shit going on in the world. Really, this is fucking bull shit breaking and entering. No one's hurt, which is a good thing, but I mean come on, newsworthy?'

'You surprise me sometimes.'

'What? What do you mean, surprise you?'

'Just, really Ricky, a man of your age. You're no fucking child, yet I don't know.' She shook her head. Her seriousness struck me as genuine and stopped me in my tracks. I continued to stare at her, but my aggression receded. Hers seemed to as well. 'You need to understand a person's psyche, what pushes

their buttons, gets them to stop and feel. What's the saying? A man's home is his castle? Yeah it's sexist, because it's the same for us woman, but the sentiment holds true. You have a home, nice things you worked hard for, a family that you've tasked yourself to love and protect. You focus your life on doing just that, then some scumbag comes into your home, your castle and threatens all that . . . I'd like to see you sleep soundly one more night of your life after that. People downplay it, the cops most of all, especially when there's no violence involved, even though there often is. My point is . . . if you want to strike a chord with Joe and Jane Public, make them itchy in their own home.' She paused. I stayed looking at her face. I hadn't seen her quite so . . . human before. I was beginning to realize I still knew absolutely zero about this girl. 'Building an audience is a slow burn.' She said. 'Remember . . . local, random and unsolved. All we're doing, is setting a foundation.'

I just blew out a breath of air I was holding in and sat back against the headrest. 'Maybe you should write the article.' I said after a minute.

She smiled. 'I'm the photographer. That's enough.'

The police cruiser turned the corner a minute later. 'Twenty eight minutes by my watch.' I said.

'Put it down and hit publish.' She said.

'You're sure?'

She nodded.

'Not sure how the cops will respond to us calling them out.'

'The louder they are, the better it is for us.' She said.

I added my last couple of sentences to really bring the point home. She started the car and pulled away. The police car slowly drove past us. Neither of us looked in their direction. I clenched my teeth and clicked 'publish'.

5

I gotta say, I was feeling really good. Whether it meant something to her or not, Veronica had made a move on me. It was brief and likely all it did was save us a hairy altercation with a couple of toughs, but nonetheless, a move was made. A door was opened that I didn't plan on closing without a fuss. Plus, I was much more at ease writing a piece without having to witness callous brutality first hand. Despite her fervent speech, a home invasion to me was much less severe than a knife to the chest or a bullet to the head. To the casual observer it is anyway.

Like all things, my victorious pride came to a screeching halt within minutes. We drove back towards Blackpool on the dark highway. The road was empty in either direction. Just a few miles out, I saw a white van pulled over at a clumsy angle on the road's shoulder. Veronica must have noticed it the same time I did because I felt the speed change as she eased off the accelerator. We approached the van at a crawl, both peering over for a glimpse. I couldn't see much in the darkness, but I thought I made out a shape behind the wheel. 'You think that's the same van?' I asked.

'I know it is.' She said. 'Well, I'm nearly certain.' She pulled the car over to the shoulder of the road in front of the van. I gave her a look that tried to convey 'You sure about this?' She gave me one back that said 'No, but I'm stopping anyway.' She kept the engine running, but pulled the emergency brake. I watched her open the door. I reached over and grabbed her arm before she could step out.

'You can come with me.' She said. 'Or not. But either way take your hand off my arm.'

I pulled my hand away. Too much too soon. I guess I misread the situation. Wasn't the first time, wouldn't be the last. After a brief personal deliberation, I opened the door and followed Veronica in a slow, hunched approach to the white van. The closer we got to the van, the clearer the scene became. I could tell the driver's door was opened slightly, I couldn't tell why. The shape behind the wheel formed into a man's figure as we approached. I paused when I saw his eyes were opened. 'He can see us.' I said.

Veronica paused when I said it. For a moment she looked unsure of herself. It was then that I noticed she was carrying a camera in her hand. It wasn't her usual enormous piece of equipment. It must have been her back up, something a little more discreet. She stood up straight. I stayed hunched down close to the barrier. 'He can't see us.' She said.

'What? He's looking right at us.'

She gave me her come on you dick look, one I was growing familiar with. 'He's dead.' She said.

'Oh.' I said. 'Shit. Isn't that worse?'

'For him it seems to be, definitely.' She said. She kept walking, with slower, shorter steps than before. I heard her mumble something.

'What's that?' I asked. She didn't look over at me, but I heard her say something like 'doesn't make sense.' I knew then this was unexpected. It wasn't something she had planned to encounter or provisioned for. She looked almost vulnerable, except her ease and lack of surprise or disgust around death still didn't jive with me. I felt my stomach churn. Even from outside the van I could smell the man's blood, taste it even, like licking a rusty knife. I was further disgusted when Veronica began taking photographs. 'What are you doing?' I asked.

'What it looks like. I'm taking pictures.'

'We're reporting on this?'

'Do you see any other choice? What, murder's not newsworthy enough for you either?'

I said nothing. 'Use your phone.' She said. 'We'll call it in. We have to now.'

'Fine.' I said. I dialed and put the phone to my ear. 'What do I tell them?'

'Tell them the truth.' She said.

So the truth is what I told them. It was fairly tactical on the phone with the dispatcher. She seemed more concerned with where I was, whether I was in danger and whether I planned to stick around. I answered explicitly to the first question and with uncertainty on the next two. A man was blatantly killed on the side of the road within the last fifteen minutes. Now I was just feet away from him on the phone to the cops and standing next to a frantic photo taker. I reckoned it was a possibility I could be clipped at any second. I hung around anyway. I had to. Veronica was my ride home and she wasn't leaving. A strange sense of calm had come over me, like I was just part of some elaborate game of clue.

We knew there were cops nearby since we'd just left a couple of uniforms outside a dark housing estate, but we weren't sure if a murder trumped a home invasion. We timed the response again. This time it was closer to seven minutes, so I guess murder gets the VIP treatment. It was brief, but it was enough time for me to type out a speculative article about stumbling across this dead body on the side of the road. The article was accompanied by a vast array of photographs of the scene provided by Veronica. I disagreed on moralistic grounds with the photos she uploaded. I found them voyeuristic. She said that was pretty much what Big Dick was going for, so this should please him no doubt. She didn't include any of the man's face, but I still felt like a mom or wife sitting around the couch, plucking through Facebook could still identify the van and accompanying body of her son or husband. At the very least it might save some cop from drawing the short straw and having to make the trip. The cops for their part were fairly brief with us. They took us for a couple just driving past. Besides taking down our contact information and verifying a few things, they didn't probe much. Still it was pretty late when we left. Veronica drove back into the city. Town was busy and she had to dodge groups of revelers along the river as she made her way towards my apartment, where she kindly dropped me off to save me a walk through one or two inner city streets worth avoiding at that hour.

I hadn't had the chance to replenish my booze supply, so my sleep was broken and nightmarish. At my desk in the morning I fought back yawns and droopy eyelids. I noticed my boss walk past my desk more often than usual, so I gathered he'd noticed my dishevel. Time would tell if he would sack up and call me out. I spent much of the morning checking our website view stats and reading the comments that started to come in quick fire succession after our post was shared a few times. As we've probably all come to expect, there is no middle ground with commenters. The first few were straight up denouncements of local law enforcement, those happy to reaffirm the incompetence of all members of the force. It was pretty much all downhill from there, but in fairness it took a good three comments before someone chimed in with outright racism. Before that, it was merely implied. This heated up by the fifth comment with the mother of all leading statements 'I'm not racist, but . . .' devolution into a three paragraph rant against immigrants ensued and I gave up reading after that, which was, in retrospect, five comments too late. I needed a laugh after that so I did a search for technological developments and found a few articles on recent smartphone software updates. I don't actually read those articles. I just scroll directly to the comments section and read firsthand the tech fan boys attack each other with many complicated words and heavily detailed, obscure references to product specifications that only an utter set of dinks can understand. They attack each other with such nerdy gusto, it's like watching Millhouse battle rap Sheldon Cooper. If you haven't given it a look, seriously, try it sometime, it's a fucking hoot.

I was smiling and chuckling to myself when the phone on my desk rang and startled me. I answered with 'Sherman here.' It was the woman from reception downstairs.

'Mr. Sherman?'

'Speaking.' I said.

'Hi, there's a gentleman here to see you, a Mr. . . .' She disappeared a moment and I could hear mumbling through the phone. I could sense her sweaty palm enclosed over the mouthpiece. 'Sorry, a Sergeant O'Brien. He's from Blackpool Police Department.' She said.

'Cops.' I thought. It could only have to do with the previous night's affair, but I racked my brain for what specifically and came up with nothing. 'I'll be down shortly.' I said.

Two unexpected visitors in as many days, although the previous day's nervous anticipation had been replaced by good old fashioned fear. I don't like the cops. I didn't then, I sure as fucking hell don't now. I walked out of the elevator and across the squeaky floor again and through the turnstile. There was only one man in reception. He was seated with a newspaper opened wide with both arms outstretched. It covered his face, but he must have heard my feet squeaking or smelled my cologne because he let a corner drop down that revealed a familiar round face with yesterday's stubble. He folded the paper and dropped it onto the table. This heavy-set man in his navy blues stood up and walked over to me. I stayed where I was, unsure of the required protocol for being summoned by an officer of the law. He held out a hand. I slowly held out my own. They touched eventually and his clammy, calloused mitt gave mine a shake. 'Hi' was all I said.

'Call me O'Brien.' He said still shaking my paw. 'Or Sergeant, whatever blows your hair back.'

'I'm Rick.'

'I know who you are.' He said. He seemed to squint and stare right through me. His eyes were too intense for the leisurely morning I had in mind for myself. 'We go somewhere to talk?' He asked. 'There's a coffee shop a few doors down.'

'Fine.' I said. Once again I followed a stranger out of the revolving door to my office building. Outside he waited for me and walked slowly beside me. He made awkward small talk about the weather and some other shit I couldn't give a fuck about. Just a few yards into the walk he pointed at the coffee shop and we headed towards it. There was an order window out front for nice days, which was opened. He ordered a couple of coffees and we sat down with them outside in the smoking area. The smell of cigarette smoke and coffee reminded me of my old man. It made me nostalgic for a time when I perceived life to be simpler and Big Dick to be less of a righteous cock. I pulled the cover off of the to-go cup and let the steam from the coffee carry the smell up my nostrils. I hoped the fumes would make me sharper instantaneously. I remember thinking it would be a great idea if a type of coffee was invented that you could just snort and get a blast of energy, then I remembered they had that already and it was called cocaine.

'I take it I'm not under arrest?' I said.

'I'm guessing you haven't been arrested before. Otherwise you'd know it doesn't typically start with a coffee and a pleasant chat. You do something that you think needs arresting over? Something wrong perhaps?'

'Wrong or illegal?'

'You find much difference between the two?'

'I don't know, I reckon I would if I thought about it.'

'Okay bud. No, you're not under arrest. You're a shit-stirrer I take it, but unfortunately there's no law against that on its own.'

I watched the man eyeball me for a few seconds. He seemed concerned with my shoulders, which I thought was weird, either that or he wasn't in the mood for eye contact. He opened a pack of cigarettes, lit one and handed one over to me along with a match.

'Well if I'm not under arrest, I guess I don't really understand your visit. The coffee's good and all, but I'm not sure it's worth it to have my entire office now thinking I've got some trouble with Johnny Law.'

'If you ask me son, I'd guess you really don't give a shit what those people in the office think. I'd wager if you did, you'd turn up in a more respectable state.'

'Oh. Okay, I get it then. You're the fashion police.' Zing I thought, lay up.

He muffled an obviously fake laugh, I found it courteous of him. 'Maybe not.' He said. 'But, I've been around a long time. Sometimes appearances can be deceiving, but most of the time they are not.'

'Okay, so I'm not enamored with my nine to five. I'm sure I'm not the first.'

'You're not, but most people just suck it up and take it until their spirit withers and their soul turns to stone. But you . . . you're different aren't you? See, I really just wanted to have a nice little chat to get to know you. That way I know you and even more importantly, you know me.'

'Fine. So you're not pissed off about my article yesterday?'

'Pissed off? No, I wouldn't say that. The rank and file aren't the ones dictating where the money's spent. That's decided over handshakes and cheap scotch still believe it or not. You want to create a little noise about response times to crimes in the rural areas, that's fine by me. See the only thing shining a light in the dark room does is that it gets cockroaches to scatter. Those with any sense leave for the next target. It's your B and C class thugs that hear some bullshit like that after its public knowledge and try to capitalize on it. Sure, we'll have a wave of amateur robberies in the next few days, but the brass will throw some cash towards overtime and beef up the units in the affected areas. Your response times will improve momentarily, some punks will get caught and knocked around then the smoke will clear. Mainstream media will paint it a success story and there you have it, back to normal everybody, business as usual.'

I sipped my coffee while he went on. I was trying to appear cool and detached, but in truth I was hanging onto every word. 'That your way of saying what I'm doing is pointless?' I asked.

He searched for an ashtray, but found none, so he stubbed out his cigarette on the plastic table. 'Not at all. Quite the opposite in fact. What you're doing is creating a stir that won't have a long term impact for us, meaning the cops that is. For you on the other hand, who knows. You made the Ouija board move, you know? You spook some here, scare some there . . . the crowd is watching. You're getting an audience, at least a start. You asked was I pissed off, well, I'm not. Intrigued is more like it.'

He seemed to settle back into his chair. He held his coffee casually with one hand, resting it on the top of his gut without making it obvious. He had the look of a man ready to launch into a harangue about kids these days. I nearly expected to hear something like 'when I was a boy . . .' Honestly, it wasn't far off that. He said 'I knew your old man way back when. You know, when we were both coming of age I guess you could put it.'

I shrugged. If I had ten cents for every windbag that told me they knew my old man way back when, I'd be rolling twenties into a ball and tossing them at strippers nine to five. 'He's still alive you know?' I said.

'I've heard. Anyway, you ever hear about how he started out, your old man?' Strangely enough I thought, I really hadn't. He'd been Big Dick, the stand-out, popular journalist since as long as I could remember. His war stories, I'd heard plenty of, but I never once sat through a tale of humble beginnings. I shook my head 'No' in response.

'I never have either.' He said. 'Funny thing about when someone gets fame or power or both, the corners they cut to get there often get lost in the noise. The ones they stepped on or double-crossed, they seem to be silenced. As they say, history's told by the winner. I believe that. Back in the day I was walking a beat. This city was a little different. Let's say it was a little more dangerous, but it was probably talked about less. Everyone just got on with it. Anyway, I ran into Dick a couple times on the way up. Seems he had a knack for reporting on stories almost the very moment they happened. An old lady might get mugged and beaten down by the canal, Big Dick would have an eyewitness source before the empty purse gets picked up down the block. A dead teenager popped outside of a barbershop in broad daylight, Big Dick would just so happened to be in the chair getting a trim. You get the point, on and on it went like that. Within a few months on the scene, he was the voice of the Blackpool beat.'

I nodded along as he spoke. I followed him sure. I was making some connections on what he was trying to say, but probably not enough. To me, he was an old man blowing smoke. I was half checked out before he began. 'That sounds great and all.' I said. 'I'm just not sure I get it yet. Is there a reason we're having this conversation?' In fairness, I was in the

mood to be obtuse.

He put his coffee onto the table along with his heavy forearms. I felt the table tense and shriek at the weight of them. His lean forward drew me in as well. I could see him clearly, in high-def. The rings around his eyes were less pronounced than say, Big Dick's, but still they were there. Neither man seemed to have aged well. 'It's a warning son. One thing about me is that I can spot patterns and for better or worse I have an elephant's memory. And when I heard about you and saw your name, well I guess you could say I got the same knot in my gut that I had all those years ago.'

I watched him slowly turn his scowl into a grimace. He pushed back in his chair and calmly stood up.

'We done here?' I asked.

He patted down his shirt and jacket and tugged his belt back into the correct spot over the center of his gut. 'For now at least.' He said. 'You remember what I said.'

I nodded and remained seated.

'Oh.' He said. 'When you see him, be sure to tell Big Dick I said hello.'

'He'll know you?'

'He's sharper than he looks. He'll remember me.'

He walked off then. I waited until I finished my coffee and then headed off. You have to consider the power of hindsight. It's potent shit. Everything in retrospect seems obvious and simple. When I lived the moment however, some thoughts were bumping around in my head sure, but I wouldn't say alarm bells were going off or anything. For the most part, I'd convinced myself he was just a cop that was a little pissed off for being called out on his shoddy work. I decided that was the root of the visit and with that a new kind of rogue confidence seemed to build up. In other words, I started to grow internet balls. Big ones. Big enough to spill over into my real life. So from that perspective, you could say that O'Brien's chat had the exact opposite impact from its intention. Go figure right? Like ninety percent of all parental advice I guess.

A few minutes later I returned to swiveling in my chair and alt-tabbing through spreadsheets and our website's stats page. The numbers were creeping up, two views a minute then three, then ten, I could feel my heart thumping with excitement in my chest. I heard a throat clear behind me and I spun around to see my bossing lurking over my shoulder. With my confidence at a new all-time high, I hadn't even bothered to flick back to the faux spreadsheet. I asked, 'What can I do for you?'

His forehead looked somewhere between nervousness and incredulity. He crouched down to be face to face with me. 'We need to talk.' He said. He pointed to a meeting room a few yards away. I shrugged 'Okay' and then stood up and followed him. He closed the door gently after I walked in. I remained standing and waiting for him to begin. I kept my back to him longer than I would have normally to look out the meeting room's window overlooking the city. He was always a nervous prick and a great man for managing upwards, so it was almost fun to watch him unravel.

'People are starting to talk.' He said.

I nodded and paused, refusing to take the initial bait. He bit down on his thumbnail and looked like a four year old. It goes to show you what a little confidence and an air of 'I don't give a shit' can do to a straight edge's comfort zone.

'About you. I mean' He continued 'showing up, stinking of booze half the time, disappearing for hours on end the other half. It doesn't look good, doesn't reflect well if you know what I mean.'

Still I gave him nothing.

'And your visitors, that . . . girl yesterday and today the police pull you out of work.'

'Damn.' I thought. I knew O'Brien's visit would jam me up. At least I figured out where the line was. 'Those are personal matters.' I said. 'They don't need to concern anybody here.'

'Fine.' He said. 'But, at work? I'm getting a lot of questions from the management team.'

'Well, you better come up with some answers.' I said.

'I better?' He asked. By this time his hands gripped his arms tightly across his chest. 'I don't think you get how this works. I'm not here to come up with answers for you. You really think that's acceptable behavior?'

I smiled. Finally the rub. Acceptable behavior said it all. Then I used my trump card. 'Your fiancé, you and her still together?'

'What?' He asked.

'You and your fiancé still together? Dark hair right?'

'Uh . . . sure okay.' He said. I watched as his feet began to shift and his hands danced from his arms to his pockets then back to his arms.'

'So you never told her about that blonde from accounting I caught you in the men's room with at that Christmas party? What was her name? Ah, it doesn't matter.'

His eyebrows grew closer together in anger at first, then dissolved into worry. 'You're blackmailing me?'

'What? Now, I didn't say anything remotely close to blackmail, did I? We're friends right? I just wanted to be sure, so I'm on top of circumstances should I ever run into her.' I gave him a closed smile and an eyebrow lift for good measure. My God, I was feeling hot. I couldn't wait to get home and flex in the mirror. 'We all set?' I asked.

He shook his head, deflated. 'We're done.' He didn't wait for me to say anything else. He left the room and disappeared back behind his desk. For all it's worth, I never would have said anything to his poor fiancé. Plus I didn't even see him with the blonde from accounting, but I did hear someone passing the information along in the coffee dock, where I sat apparently invisible choking down an instant coffee. Honestly, I didn't mind the guy, but I wasn't about to let the company stop paying me without exhausting all my options. That was pretty

much the only chip I was holding.

6

It was dark by the time I found myself standing in Harlot's Lane yet again. I was there to meet Veronica for our next assignment. I paused halfway between her doorway and that of Harlot's Den. I almost walked into the bar out of habit at this stage to seek out Big Dick, but I thought better of it at the last moment. I was feeling confident and I wanted that to last as long as possible. If Big Dick had any strengths besides drinking, it was his ability to make me feel downtrodden and suicidal within moments of striking up a conversation. Based on that inevitable outcome, I shuffled my feet over to Veronica's door again. Once again my knock left the downstairs door ajar. I walked into the hallway. The bulb dangled as before although the flicker appeared to have grown worse, its increased frequency giving the cheesy haunted house effect to the entrance and stairwell. I reached the top of the stairs and paused to listen for murmured voices, but heard nothing this time. I knocked on the door. It was a man's knock, a confident set of knuckles if I do say so myself. I stood contemplating her reaction to such a masculine rap of the fist's back. I heard footsteps from the other side of the door and adjusted my stance to match it with the testosterone fueled beckon. A tall man with broad shoulders opened the door and nearly put me into a roll down the stairs. I grunted like a man sucker-punched in his gut. It was not my finest split-second.

'Oh, sorry.' The man said.

I waved him off. 'It's okay.' I squeaked through a cleared throat.

'I didn't hear anyone knock. My bad.'

'Bastard.' I thought. 'Is someone there?' I heard Veronica yell. Her footsteps echoed from her apartment through the bare hallway. I saw why when I saw her wearing boots with aggressive stiletto heels. 'Ricky?' She said. 'Why didn't you knock?'

'I . . . uh, I was about to.' I said.

The man said. 'Sorry again buddy. Take care Veronica.'

I nodded and so did Veronica. The man then left.

I looked to her for an explanation, but received none. 'Give me a second.' She said. She disappeared back into her apartment. I stood in the hall trying to make out the wording of the prayer attached to her crucifix at the end of the corridor, but the writing was tough to read from far away. It looked like Chinese characters, which I thought was strange. She appeared a moment later with her bag. I went to step into the corridor, but she put a hand to my chest and pushed me back into the hall. 'We're leaving.' She said. She closed the door behind her and locked the top latch with her key.

'But, your car?'

'We're not taking my car tonight.'

'Walking somewhere?'

She rolled her eyes. 'Just follow me.' She said.

Yet another handsome, well turned out male visitor, she could've been leading me anywhere, for the first few minutes I followed blindly while my mind raced to some weird and wild places. I did what I could to rationalize, cable guy, Jehovah's witness, boiler repair man, extremely dapper plumber, nothing seemed to fit. Insurance salesman maybe, but not likely. Every step she took those boots clucked off of the concrete like horse hooves in a parade. A half-mile away I couldn't take it any longer. The clucking was my own *Tell Tale Heart*, I could carry on without an explanation no longer. I stopped. A few steps later, Veronica noticed. She stopped and spun towards me. The twist of her boot heel made a shrieking noise when she turned. 'Problem?' She asked. She looked young and helpless in the streetlight's glare. I knew better. She also looked irritated.

'You get many visitors?' I asked.

'Do I get many visitors? What the hell is your deal?' She shook her head and rolled her eyes. Then she turned and continued walking, or trotting more like it.

I jogged to catch up. She didn't slow down. 'Wait.' I said. I put my hand on her arm to stop her. She paused and looked at my hand, then followed my arm up past my shoulder to my face. 'It's just that . . . those guys at your place yesterday, then today, again . . . I guess I just . . .'

'Do we really need to have another boundaries discussion?'

I slowly shook my head.

'Good.' She said.

I said 'Fine.' I was defeated.

'Can we go now?' She asked. I held my hand out

to indicate I was good with that suggestion. It began raining and the wind picked up. Debris from the unkempt gutters blew out into the street. Empty bags of potato chips stayed airborne the longest, their landing place dictated by the rhythm of the wind. It felt more like autumn than a summer's evening. We walked by crowded bus stops and bars where revelers spilled out onto the sidewalk from the smoking area as we continued along the riverfront. Veronica received catcalls while we past, courtesy of her provocative footwear I guessed. She ignored them. I did my best not to look intimidated, by her or them. Outside of one bar, a guy slapped me on the back as I walked by as if to say 'nice work champ.' I smiled and carried on. We reached a set of traffic lights at a heavy intersection. Veronica led me north away from the river. The noise from the cars and people along the river grew faint as we walked. A few twists and turns later and we entered a long pedestrian street. The road was quiet except for the bass-heavy music coming from an apartment window and the noise of a baby crying from somewhere. We were in an area I'd heard of plenty of times, but only enough to make a mental note to stay out of it. When the realization hit me, I stopped walking again.

'What now?' She asked.

'Come on Veronica, you know what. What the fuck are doing here? I know where we are. I gotta say, I don't feel safe.'

'Well I gotta say Ricky, you're probably not. If you know where you are, then you know enough to keep moving.'

'Yeah, but where are we going? I didn't sign on to get killed before I'm even started.'

'Settle down. We're going to a contact's house. A friend. Where's your sense of adventure?'

'It's out of practice. You have a contact? Here?'

'Come on.' She said. She led the way up a set of concrete steps. She tried the doorknob. It twisted and the door opened into a dim hallway. The was a door to the left and right and a set of stairs at the back. The hall was bare except for a radiator that lined one wall. It was chipped and rusted and looked dangerous. Veronica walked over to the door on the right. She knocked loudly. My heart started beating quickly. I could feel it in my temples. 'I'll do the talking.' She said.

I muttered something along the lines of 'No shit.'

On the other side of the door I heard the click of metal locks being undone. The door creaked open slowly. It caught on the latch that was left connected. A short Latino woman peaked out from the opening. She looked young, low twenties I guessed. Her hair was pulled back tightly, her lips were pursed and uninviting. She glared at Veronica and looked her up and down. She may have glared at me, I'm not sure. Either way, I was dismissed as a threat with barely a moment's thought. 'You lost?' She asked through the crack.

Veronica shook her head. 'Here for Green Peter.' She said. 'He's expecting us.' The woman didn't say anything back. She kept her eyes on Veronica a few seconds longer then closed the door. I heard locks being reattached on the other end and had to purposely stop myself commenting on the potential fire safety issue. When the door was closed I asked Veronica 'Green Peter?'

'Pedro Verde.' She said. 'Friend of a friend.'

His demotion from a friend to a friend of a friend was not lost on me. I didn't probe. I figured the truth was less again.

'He's active in a few different causes.' She said.

'Oh.' I said. 'Okay.' Obviously unclear as to her meaning or its relevance to our situation.

'He's also really dangerous.' She said. 'And, from

what I've heard, he's not that fond of white guys. Try to avoid pissing him off.'

It was a vote of confidence if I've ever received one. I heard the locks chiming again behind the door. I swallowed saliva and made an exaggerated sound that drew a glare from Veronica. 'Just getting it out of the way.' I said.

The door opened fully this time. A man stood staring at the two of us. He looked older than I had expected. It was probably racist of me, but when she said Green Peter I had in my head a gangbanger, someone you mind find in the wrong part of LA. This man was not that. He was in good shape, I could tell, dare I say sinewy. He looked more black than Hispanic to me, but I didn't journey down that line of questioning. He held his hand out to Veronica first and smiled. 'I'm Peter.' He said. Veronica shook his hand. 'Thanks for having us.'

'My pleasure.' He said. He held his hand out to me next. 'You must be the writer's son. Sherman right?'

'I am. Call me Rick.' I said.

'Good. Well come in.'

We walked in behind him. I shut the door afterwards, but decided it wasn't my place to bother with the locks. He sat us down in a quaint living room. It had large windows with views up and down the block. There were family photos on the wall and fresh carpet. I was comfortable. It was homey and I liked it. I stood at the window and peered down the street. It was still empty, but it looked less ominous from inside the cozy sitting room. I heard Veronica and Green Peter talking quietly in the doorway that led to the kitchen. I heard laughter and pleasantries being exchanged. After a minute he said 'I'll leave you to it.' And then he left. Veronica walked over and sat on the couch. She began taking her camera and laptop out of her bag. I sat next to her and took the laptop to start it up.

'Well?' I said. 'I presume there's a plan.'

'There is.'

'You want to fill me in?'

She continued adjusting the camera. She walked over to the window and began pointing the camera out towards the street, testing its range through the glass. 'We're broadening our demographic.' She said.

'What, like . . . the black community?'

She looked at me then shook her head. 'No, well, not really . We're not telling them anything they don't already know.'

'So who then?'

She thought about it for a few seconds before answering. 'Sympathetic white people I guess. That's the best way to put it, or you could say the left leaning population, young, college educated, that type of thing. We're going to give them a glimpse of how the cops treat the other half.'

'Okay.' I said. It seemed as good a cause as any, but something didn't sit right with me. 'I'm all for this Veronica, but I have to say, it sounds odd this direction coming from Big Dick. He's not what I'd call a racial bridge builder.'

Veronica smiled. 'Maybe you're not as dumb as you pretend to be.'

I smiled, mostly because I wasn't pretending to be anything. 'So this is you, you're doing, not Big Dick's?' I knew she had an angle in this, it wasn't a hundred percent clear as of yet, but the dust was coming off of it.

She nodded. 'Big Dick wanted us on the riverfront to catch junkies sticking up tourists.'

'And?'

'We'll get to it if there's time.'

'But that's more of the same. Right?'

She nodded. 'It is. Dick knows journalism or at

least he did. For the life of him he doesn't get technology. The game has changed. If we stick with only one demographic now, we're stuck with it. Online searches, social media, it's all rigged to give you more of what your browser history says you like. We'll be pigeon-holed immediately out of the box. We need to keep the algorithms guessing for now. You get it?'

'You seem to, I'll leave it at that.' I was still bullshit at Big Dick for three decades of being an asshole, so I didn't mind riding this out. 'Your technology, or data whatever tell you something's likely to go down here tonight.'

She laughed. 'No. We don't need data for this one. It's a nightly occurrence.'

At that, we set to it. She opened up a number of folders on the laptop and told me to read through what was in them to put together some background. There were mountains of information in each folder, daily logs, video feeds, copies of police reports. I could've spent a month digesting everything in them. She informed me that I had at least an hour, maybe two. The information was Green Peter's. He appeared to be a collector and a good one at that. Veronica said it was all research that was going into his upcoming

book. I thought it was weird that he was okay with us preempting the topic, but Veronica again pointed to the demographic. If anything, we were advertising his work to a new audience.

I researched, wrote and rewrote flat out for two hours. It felt like ten minutes. I only stopped when I ran a forearm across my forehead and caught sight of a clock above the oven in the kitchen. I thought it might be frozen and wrong, but the minute hand changed as I watched it and the corner of the laptop screen confirmed the same. I finished up the paragraph I was tweaking and hit save. Something felt wrong. I could hear the television on in another room and somewhere a clock ticked seconds away, a noise that would have irked me had I noticed it earlier. I looked over at Veronica. She sat on her thigh on the window sill. She hadn't moved in quite some time, not enough for me to take notice anyway. Her eyes were squinted and she chewed on her bottom lip enough to leave it red raw underneath. She sensed me watching her and looked over.

'Something doesn't feel right.' I said.

She pulled her thigh off of the window sill and stood up. 'No. You're right. Something is off. You hear that?'

I listened for a few seconds and then shook my head.

'Exactly.'

Someone swore loudly in the next room. The actual words were muffled by the wall, but it was enough to draw attention from both of us. I heard footsteps seconds later, then the door to the next room swung open. 'You're gonna want to see this.' He said to both of us. He turned to walk back into the next room. Veronica and I followed.

In the next room, the girl that answered the door sat drinking tea on the couch. Her eyes were fixed on the television screen. When I looked I could see why. It was a breaking news report. A local reporter stood in front of the Blackpool River. I could see yellow tape and flashing police sirens that distorted the scene behind the talking head. A banner scrolled at the bottom of the screen. It read "Mass shooting on the boardwalk. Developing: Details to follow." I could see figures moving in and out of view in the background. I walked closer to the television for a better look. I could hear Peter speaking to Veronica, but I wasn't listening as I focused on the screen. A familiar shape came into focus. I squinted for a better look and took one step closer. I reached out to touch the screen with

my index finger. As I did, the familiar shape turned his head. O'Brien, the cop that paid me a visit, appeared to look directly at me. I got an eerie sense that by some magic he could see through the camera lens and focus on me directly. I swore he looked at me and smiled. 'I know him.' I said. The others grew quiet and looked at me. I was suddenly aware of my awkwardness and my finger resting on the screen. Veronica shot me a look that I read at first as curious and then panicked. I made eye contact with Green Peter. The two hours of intensive research into an anti-police indictment occurred to me. I voiced the first thing that came to my head. 'I mean, I remember him from when my old man was doing investigative work still . . .' I trailed off as I watched Green Peter's face chew through a few thoughts.

He looked at Veronica. 'I can get you close, but not too close.'

Veronica nodded. 'I understand.' She said.

Green Peter grabbed a set of car keys from a dish on the coffee table. He led us out to the street where he was parked. He dropped us a block away from the crime scene on the boardwalk a couple of minutes later. Veronica thanked him and assured him we'd still run a story on his work. It sounded forced to me.

I wondered what promises she'd already made to this guy. I climbed out of the back seat and said a curt good bye. I received a similar response in return. I had to jog to keep up with Veronica as she headed towards the commotion. A crowd had gathered around the area. Veronica weaved through spaces I was unable to negotiate. I shoved my way past to stay close to her, but before long she was lost in the sea of faces. I was caught up in the tightening crowd that restricted my movements to the rolling wave-like motion of an open sea. I strained to see past the police tape. In doing so, I unexpectedly made eye contact with O'Brien. This time it was no illusion. He saw me for certain and my presence was registered in his mind, I just knew it. I looked away quickly and scanned the rest of the perimeter. I eventually spotted the frizzy ball of hair that gave Veronica away. She made it down to the front and stood speaking with a policeman and someone from the news crew. The conversation looked animated. I was too far away to hear voices and not crafty enough to read lips. A minute later she was gone. I missed her exit due to an untimely blink. I picked up the moving ball of frizz again as it made its way back through the crowd and emptied out on the opposite side of the street. I

pushed my way out again and headed after her.

I glanced back at the chaos behind me and noticed for the first time covered shapes lying motionless on the ground amongst the policemen's feet. I grew lightheaded. I counted five shapes before I looked away. I felt ready to vomit as I continued after Veronica. My mind was racing and everything and anything bounced around in there. I hurried across a street and a car nearly took me out of it. I jumped back just in time. The shock must have jolted a memory loose. Puzzled thoughts began sticking to each other in my head. First O'Brien's words of warning, next Veronica's throw away comment earlier 'Big Dick wanted us on the riverfront.' I felt goosebumps up both arms. Life offers very few actual coincidences. Everything else is either by design or an unintended result of that design. I no longer needed to catch up with Veronica, who seemed to be one of those women with an unnaturally quick walking pace. It was obvious now that she put some pieces together quicker than I had. She was going after Big Dick. What she would do when she got there only time would tell. At that time I figured anything he got, he deserved.

I began to think about how Big Dick might react

to being confronted. His reaction to challenges proved inconsistent across history. He was equal parts lethargic nonchalance and Incredible Hulk. I decided I should keep moving quickly just in case. I thought Veronica had lost me, but a minute later I could hear the crack of her stiletto heels off of the concrete. Even if I couldn't see her due to twists and turns, her trail of echo let me know I was close. Her footsteps ceased about the same time a waft of sewage creeped up my nostrils. I turned the corner to see the neon sign for the Harlot's Den. As I approached, the door pushed open and a man with shock white hair stepped out. He had a cigarette between his lips already. When he held a lighter to his face I recognized him before the puff of white smoke clouded my view. It was the Editor in Chief of the *Blackpool Daily*, well, the former I should say. In other words, the man that oversaw the downfall of a journalistic stalwart, the voice of a nation, the words of saints and hero's, and blah blah fucking blah. Let's just call him Chief. He'd like that anyway.

'You looking for me Chief?' I asked.

He took a long haul from his cigarette and blew smoke directly over my head with squinted eyes and crow's feet. 'Sherman?'

'That's right.' I said.

He pulled his cigarette from his mouth with this left hand, smiled and held out his right. 'How the hell are ya kid? I was in giving your old man shit that's all. He's an anachronism you know? Sees it one way and only one way. Won't change for anyone's sake not least his own.'

His amenable disposition startled me. My working theory on the situation at the time, albeit changing by the second, was that this man had threatened to bury me, thus driving Big Dick to lend a helping hand on my behalf. Slowly I reached my hand out and shook his. 'Anachronism, he is that definitely. I think he's always been that, even during his own time. You know, for spite's sake.' I decided to test the waters with this guy. From what I recalled, he wasn't that good a bullshit artist. 'This a courtesy call on Dick?'

He laughed like I laid down a solid knock knock joke. Slowly he pulled himself together. 'No son. I don't think there is such a thing with your old man. He wanted to talk business. Said he wanted to bring me in on something big, provided I brought along some of my old contacts in the ad business. By the time I showed up he was angry and drunk, I don't

know which happened first, but he didn't want to hear a word I had to say. Tried telling him the game has changed you know. You go digital, fine, that's where the world's going today, but soon as you do, you aren't competing for advertising dollars with other newspapers and magazines, you're going toe to toe with Google and Facebook and whoever else comes along next.'

I nodded along as he spoke and kept a smile on my face, which masked an endless array of 'what the fucks?' knocking around my interior.

He just continued talking. 'Most people don't want news anymore.' He said. 'At least not any news with depth. Everything is lists, bullet points, videos, so on and so on. You've got aggregators ripping off news from publishers, not giving them a dime. It's dog eat dog, even more than used to be. If you ask me, the decline in human attention span is much more worrying than a drop in the number of newspapers being sold. Companies come and go. Ours had a good long run. I said pretty much the same to your Dad. He kept going on about getting back to basics like the old days, whatever the hell that means. I don't think he even had a clue what I was talking about.'

I smiled and nodded. 'I can just about guarantee he didn't.' I said.

He finished his cigarette and flicked it into the gutter at my feet. 'Anyway, I need to be heading off.' He said. 'You take care of yourself okay Rick.'

I stopped him gently with a hand on his chest. 'Wait . . . Chief, about everything, we're good you and I?'

He slapped me hard on the arm and laughed. He kept his hand gripped on my shoulder. 'Son, I used to get woken up most nights by frantic phone calls. An old machine would break down at the print press and it'd be so old, we couldn't get parts to fix it. A journalist would go missing for days, miss a deadline, have a worried wife chewing her nails off, calling me looking for answers. Since we shut down, I've been in bed by ten every night and not up until eight in the morning at the very earliest. I mean, that's every day. I've lost weight, I walk, I golf, hell, I'm having sex with my goddamn wife again.' He took his hand off my shoulder and straightened my collar. 'Let me ask you, would you rather die slowly or go out in a flash?'

'Me? Probably neither.'

He laughed. 'Good answer. The Daily got its death sentence the day the first iPhone released. If

anything, you just helped it along. And in doing so . . . I think you probably saved my life.'

He smiled and gave me a mock salute. Then he walked away. I watched him turn the corner. Yet again, I felt like I had more questions than answers. Regardless, his words were redemption, a weight lifted off of my shoulders and I felt freedom. I put my hand on the door and pushed in. My old friend anxiety came quickly crawling back into my shoulders. I expected to hear yelling or at least raised voices belonging to Veronica and Big Dick. Instead there was silence. The guy with the biceps was sweeping up what sounded like broken glass behind the bar. He gave me a brief look then returned to his push broom. There was no music playing and the lights were brighter than any previous visit. The place looked run down in the dark. It looked derelict in the light. Dive or not, there was no masking the aftermath of an argument. Broken glasses and knocked over stools paved the way towards the back bar.

As I walked, my stomach turned questionable once again. Flashes of bodies lined out on the boardwalk played in my mind. Glimpses of previously unregistered details worked their way to my memory. The details grew so vivid it was difficult to tell what

was seen and what my brain added after the fact. Pooled blood and bare feet, an errand flip flop, discarded bullet casings, yellow triangles laid by the police marking evidence for the investigation, each blink of the eye carried with it a compilation of accessories. I stepped gently through the mess of the front bar room, bracing myself for what lay beyond it. I half expected to be greeted with another gruesome scene of violence and blood. I wondered had Big Dick bought it in the end. Veronica with her small quick hands and sharp blade, I didn't know her well enough to guess whether she'd lash out to her mentor if pushed far enough. I imagined she wouldn't hesitate, but time would tell. Then I got wobbly knees considering whether maybe she wasn't quick enough and Big Dick's anger and girth squashed her like a bug on the windshield. Luckily when I turned the corner, it looked less impacted than the front. Big Dick sat alone at his corner of the bar. There was an open bottle of fireball whiskey next to his arm. His gorilla mitt gripped a high ball glass. He didn't look up when I entered the room. I walked over to him. The stench of booze was either from him or the open bottle, my guess was him. His cheeks were red like he wore blush and his neck was blotchy. His snout

looked larger than usual and spit flew out of his mouth as he muttered to himself. He finally turned to look at me when I sat down next to him.

'Where's Veronica?' I asked.

He laughed. It was wet and maniacal.

'Dad?' I said. He waved his arm at me and I ducked. The flailed limb bounced weakly off of my forearm.

'Bah.' He said. 'I'll tell you where she's not. She's not where I told her to be. And you . . .' He said. He pointed a calloused index finger towards my chest. He could barely hold his arm up. The raised finger looked to be drawing slow circles. 'You're just as bad. Following that piece of tail around like a lost puppy. Instead of listening to your own father.'

I couldn't help but laugh. 'We'll work it through Veronica. I think that's pretty much what you said to me isn't it?'

He paused. I could tell my remark registered, though he wasn't one for apologizing at the best of times. He put his glass down and grabbed the bottle of fireball. He held it out to me. I waved him off and he poured what was left into his glass. 'She said her piece and stormed off.'

'She's upstairs?'

He shrugged. 'When one storms off, they don't typically announce their destination.'

I felt better now knowing she had come and gone even if I wasn't sure where she headed next. The best thing really would've been to leave then myself, but there was more I needed to know. 'I ran into Chief outside.' I said.

Big Dick pulled his hat from his head and ran a hand through his stringy silver hair. 'Another fucking bollocks.' He said. Spit flew from his mouth when he said it. He gulped down half of his fireball before continuing. 'Come in here and can't shut up about big fucking data and content this, content that. Sounded just like Veronica. A real fucking bollocks. Useless fucker. He's forgotten how the game is played.'

'I don't know Dad. Might be he's just trying to tell you the game has changed.'

He looked at me with the same expression that Caesar gave Brutus. It was disgust, surprise and defeat all in one. He turned it into a scowl a second later. 'The game has changed? The game is the same Little Dick. The players might be different, the technology more advanced, but believe this, the same shit sells today that sold in my day and a hundred

years before that. Violence, sex, fear . . . you hear me? That is it.'

I wasn't sure he was wrong all of a sudden. I mean, of course he was wrong to a degree, but he wasn't off by much. Violence, sex, fear. I repeated it several times in my head. A self supporting triangle. He might be past his sell-by date, but Big Dick saw a thing or two in his day and what he was saying was nothing revolutionary. Good news was no news. He's been feeding that line to me for over thirty years. Deep down I knew it to be the truth. Big Dick covered the Trade Center in ninety-three. He told me how the phones were ringing off the hook after the bomb went off, supermarkets and car dealers looking for ad space in the next print run. It sickened me then and it does now. Commerce has no morals, only sales targets and shareholders. I decided to switch tact. There was no use confronting him about motives, about lying to me over the *Blackpool Daily* gunning for me. As clear as Big Dick is on what sells newspapers, I'm doubly clear on what motivates Big Dick. That's money and fame, in that order. And since he placed himself hidden in the background on this project, that takes fame out of the equation. So money it is. 'We're through with this huh?' I asked.

He looked at me sternly for a few seconds. He looked like he was trying to focus through the fog. 'You do what you need to do. You and Veronica want to go save the world, then go save the fucking world. As for me, I'm out.'

'What are you gonna do?'

'I'm gonna disappear. You might consider doing the same.'

'Disappear . . . is that out of want or need?'

'I'm not one who's going to stick around and find out.' He said.

'I got a visit from someone you used to know. A cop called O'Brien.'

Big Dick put his glass down and kept both hands folded around it.

'He told me some things. A story . . . about when you first started coming up. It's not so hard to do the math.'

'Don't worry about O'Brien.' He said.

'You don't worry about him, fine. But a cop comes poking around me, I get a little worried. Especially considering tonight.'

'He came and saw you tonight?'

'He didn't come and see anything. He spotted me in a crowd. Me. Among maybe a hundred people, he lays his focus on me. Those curious eyes and fat face.'

'Listen kid. Stay out of his way, answer his questions if he grabs you, do what you got to do. I'm saying don't worry about him though. My guy's the best in the business.'

'Your guy?'

'Yeah my fucking guy. My fixer.'

'Fixer? So it's true?' I asked. I didn't need to. Of course it was true. He didn't bother answering the question, just continued.

'Half Spanish, half Hawaiian. This guy can look Black, Arab, Jew, Chinese, fucking Irish, it doesn't matter. Give him the right time of day, right lighting and some lead time on the facial hair, cops will be sketching anything from Charlie Brown to Jimi Hendrix. He's a pro too.'

I wish I could say I was surprised. I wasn't though. Not even in the slightest. My motor functions began to operate on their own. I felt blood pulsing through my ears. Big Dick continued to talk, but I stopped listening. I didn't want to hear it and I didn't want to know any of it. The more I knew, the more I had to lose. I got out of my seat and leaned on the chair for a minute to catch my breath. Big Dick finally

stopped talking. All I could hear now through the pulsing was his breathing. His cinnamon whiskey breath clung to my nose hairs. I savored the aroma as the last particle of scent from Big Dick that I ever planned to inhale. A few seconds later, I left.

7

I went to work early the next day. It was easily my most productive professional morning in close to a decade. I wrote up several reports that had hung over me for weeks and months. I returned phone calls, replied to emails, acknowledged the presence of my colleagues. It was a flash back to my early days before my ambition flamed out. I managed to clear a month long backlog of work in three focused hours. By noon, I was caught up. Believe that? Three hours of actual effort and I produced more work than the previous entire month. I laughed to myself over a cup of instant coffee in the kitchen afterwards. It spoke volumes about large companies and the inefficient bureaucracy many had become. It was a weakness I felt compelled, even required to exploit. I looked out over the city from a chair in the kitchen. I had avoided looking at the news. I wasn't ready to learn the details. I knew I was an unwitting accomplice, but no amount of self convincing allowed me to expel the guilt that burrowed into my gut. I hadn't heard from Veronica yet either. She obviously had to know what Big Dick had done. How long she knew or at least suspected was a different question. I sensed it was one with a much more complicated answer. It was an answer I both wanted to know and hoped to avoid.

I got up from my seat and poured the dregs of my coffee down the sink. I ran the faucet for a few seconds. The running water muffled the opening door so that when I turned and saw my boss a yard away from me, it was as if he dropped from the sky. His breathing was loud like he took the stairs instead of the elevator and his face was concerned.

I pulled a paper towel off the roll and wiped splashed water from my hands. 'You all right?' I asked.

He took in a deep breath. 'Yeah, I'm fine. Ran up the last couple flights. Listen, he's back.'

'What?' I asked. 'Who's back? Fucking Elvis?'

'That fat cop from the other day. He's downstairs in reception. He's got a few boys in blue with him too.'

'Shit.' I said. 'Don't let him up.'

'I don't plan to.'

'You don't?'

'Fuck no. It's clear he isn't dropping in for a chat.'

'Thanks. I mean, thanks for the tip off.' I was surprised. I felt guilty for threatening to blackmail the poor sap.

'Yeah. Listen, man. I don't know what's going on. I know we're not having a great run, but . . . we were friends once you know.'

I nodded. He was right, I had to admit it. There was a time when we were friends. Being honest, he was probably still the same guy. It was more me that took a turn. I saw the light I guess. Or the darkness. Either way. 'I guess this is the end for me here.' I said. It wasn't a question.

'Anything you can't leave behind?'

I shook my head. 'I can't head out the front.' I said.

He reached into his pocket and pulled out a set of keys. He struggled with the set for a few seconds and finally pulled off a small key. Take the emergency exit, back stairs. 'Here.' He said and handed over the key. 'Take my bike, it's a blue fold up one chained to the gate out back.'

I took the key from his hand and stuffed it into my pocket. 'Thanks.' I said again.

'Go.' He said.

I left the kitchen and walked directly towards the emergency exit. The push door emptied into a bare stairwell. The door slammed closed behind me and echoed loudly. I made my way down quickly. I breathed in sawdust and paint fumes as I descended. There were several flights and I was nearly out of breath towards the bottom. My hamstrings were burning when I reach the final landing. The exit door emptied out at the side of the building. I ran over to a line of bicycles locked to a rack. I saw the little fold up bike. I unlocked the chain, but I struggled to get the thing unfolded and upright. I heard footsteps and voices approaching. I saw long shadows stretch out over the cement as a group of people rounded the building. I was sweating with the effort and decided to ditch the bike. I gave it a good kick for its trouble, then started to run. I heard someone call out and a series of footsteps take off in a run behind me. It could've been anyone, but I didn't bother to look back. I turned down a narrow side street that emptied out along the river. I slowed to a jog at first then a

brisk walk as I entered the pedestrian traffic as nonchalantly as a man sweating through his suit can manage. I heard someone call out again. This time it was clearly my name that was called. I definitely heard 'Sherman'. I ducked my head deeper into my shoulders and quickened my stride. A large group walked past me moving in the opposite direction. I used the cover to chance a look back. I could see it was definitely two police officers coming after me. They appeared to be following as opposed to really giving chase. There's a difference, believe me. I saw no sign of O'Brien, but that didn't surprise me since he didn't look the type to bother with a foot race. I was coming up to a bridge that crossed the river. I was preparing to turn onto the bridge and take off running again. Before I could, a black Mercedes pulled to the curb and the door swung open. The window was open and I recognized the man looking out from it. 'Sherman, get in.' He said.

I paused. I tilted my head and kept looking at him. There was a man in the back that had pushed the door open. I peaked in, I recognized him also. They were two of the men I bumped into in Veronica's hallway. I glanced back quickly. There was a crowd of pedestrians obstructing the view, but I

thought I could still see the cops walking after me. I turned back and slid into the back seat. The moment I did, the car took off. The acceleration pushed me back into the seat and the door slammed shut. The window rolled up and it was tinted dark. I knew if the cops didn't see me get in, they'd not be able to see me now. I turned to look back. A hand slapped my chest and I looked forward. The guy next to me said. 'Don't give them a reason to get suspicious.'

I nodded. 'You think they saw me get into the car?'

'Unlikely.' The man driving said. 'You didn't hesitate long.'

'If they did, they might run the plates.' I said. 'That an issue for either of you?'

The man next to me answered. 'It's his car.' He pointed to the driver. 'There's nothing to hide here. They wouldn't have seen the plates, but not a big deal if they did.'

'Not a big deal? They obviously wanted to arrest me.'

'Did you sleep in your apartment last night?'

'What? Yeah, of course.'

'If they had something to arrest you on, they would have picked you up last night, don't you think?'

I didn't answer right away. I guessed this stranger was right, but honestly I didn't know what to think. I also didn't feel comfortable brain storming potential legal avenues with these two handsome callers that appeared out of the blue to grab me. Then a thought occurred to me. I considered how to phrase it. 'If they have nothing on me, then why would Veronica send you guys to scoop me up at all?' I watched them exchange glances in the rearview mirror.

'Ask her yourself when you see her.' The driver said.

'Fine.' I said. That confirmed for me who sent these men and where they were taking me. Although as we turned onto a leafy street with a row of large Georgian houses I became confused. There were names of countries and various flags on half of the houses we past. It was known as embassy row, home to ambassadors of oil-rich states and the odd billionaire. We turned into a driveway and a large gate opened to let us pass through. The Mercedes slowly passed over a gravel path, through a metal barrier to a parking lot underneath the residence. The man driving got out and opened the back door for me. I got out slowly and looked around. They led me over to an elevator.

'Who the fuck are we visiting, Tony Stark?' I asked. Both men smiled at me. One of them said 'Take the elevator to the first floor, then get out and walk up the stairs. There's a room a few doors down on the left. The door will be open, Veronica's up there waiting for you.'

I looked at them both. 'You're not coming with me?' Each shook his head. 'Okay.' I said. I walked into the lift and pressed the button for the first floor. The elevator was slow and noisy. At the first floor, the door chimed and slid open slowly like it needed grease. I walked out into a large foyer. It could've been a hotel lobby. There were paintings on the walls and ornate furniture scattered around the room. Half of the furniture had white sheets draped over it. My footsteps echoed off the tall ceiling. The house had a musty smell and I noticed cracks in the walls and chipped paint on the ceiling after my eyesight adjusted to the hazy interior. Dust came off the bannister onto my hand as I walked up the stairway. The second floor looked just as big as the first. Several doors lined each wall. I followed the hallway down until I reached the first opened doorway. I paused and looked into the room. There was an old mahogany desk. It sat bare except for an opened laptop in front of an empty chair. I walked in further. I heard the squeak of furniture and turned to see Veronica. Her neck was turned to look at me and she smiled. She sat in a wooden rocking chair facing out the window to an overgrown garden behind the house.

'Hey.' She said. She turned the rocking chair to face my direction. I pulled a chair from underneath the desk and sat down across from her.

'I half expected to find the bad guy and his cat from Inspector Gadget.' I said.

'Well Ricky, I'm sorry to disappoint.'

'You're a close second.'

'Thanks. I think.' She reached across and nudged the laptop on the desk closer to me. I looked at the screen. Our website was up and I quickly read the first paragraph of the article I wrote for Green Peter.

'You published it anyway?' I asked.

Veronica nodded her head 'Yes.' She reached over and ran her finger across the mouse pad. She brought up the stats page. I could see the spike in the bar graph that showed the number of unique visitors. 'That's not too bad.' I said.

'It's not the worst. Green Peter's network was

ready up to promote the piece. Mine was too. I used Peter's earlier videos clips, just kept the reference vague. After Big Dick's showing last night, we were always going to be second billing today.'

I nodded my head. 'You know it was Big Dick then? I mean, his . . . guy.'

'I do. I guess I always knew the score, or suspected it at least.'

'You stuck around anyway? Got into business with him?'

Veronica shrugged. 'I have a few things to say to the world. Big Dick has a big name. I needed it.'

'You got me instead?'

'You've got the same name don't you?'

'I guess.'

'Plus it wasn't me that brought you in.'

'No?'

She reached into a drawer and pulled out a large brown envelope. She took out its contents and handed them across to me. They were photographs, A4 size. They were of me. 'I'm sorry Ricky. You were his fall guy.' She said. I flipped through the photos. Each one was of me from a slightly different angle, the distance between the camera and my face closing in with each photo taken. It was from the first day together, at the park. The day the hipster got knifed and the man responsible got himself clipped. I thought about it for a few seconds and knew then with certainty that Big Dick sent his fixer out and he had to have been the one to pull the trigger. I guessed he probably paid off the drug addict first to start something with the crowd of guys, then took him out to close the loop. The photos put me at the same location.

'You took these.' I said.

'Big Dick has copies. It was his request.'

'What good are they to him? Lot of people were at that park that day.'

'Yeah, but come on. You're at the park just before an attack and a murder go down. Next day you're at another crime scene giving a statement, then last night. That cop you know?'

'O'Brien.' I said.

'Yeah him. He made you last night, correct? That's three crime scenes in quick succession.'

'It's all bullshit though. Coincidence.'

'It's not though.'

I thought about it a few seconds more. 'No, you're right, it's not.'

'It doesn't look good.'

'But?'

'But, what? There's no but, it just doesn't look good that's all.'

'Maybe not, but not looking good still isn't a crime. There's no evidence I did anything wrong.'

'No there's not. If there was, you would've been in handcuffs today.'

'O'Brien came looking for me. But you already knew that. '

'He has nothing on you. Just some circumstantial bullshit. But I'm sure he has plenty of questions.'

'Well, so do I.'

She shook her head. 'You can't be talking to this guy Ricky. Say one wrong thing and he'll get you. And you'll probably sink me in it while you're at it.'

'So that's why you scooped me up? You're afraid I'm gonna get popped and take you down.'

'Just a precaution.' She said.

'Well he's looking for me. What do you suggest I do?'

'There are a few options. Best one is you stay here for a while. Let things cool down.'

'Here? Like here, here? This house.'

'Not big enough?'

'It's plenty roomy. It's just, well, what the fuck is this place?'

'It's just a house. A big empty one.'

'Okay, who's house.'

'I guess you could say it's mine.'

'Yours?' I asked. She nodded her head.

'Dare I ask how you acquired such an estate?'

'My father bought it just before the world's financial systems imploded.'

'Why doesn't he live here?'

'Because once the economy tanked and he realized he paid way above the new market value for this gaudy piece of shit his heart exploded.'

I didn't know how to respond. I remained silent for a few seconds. I was trying to respect the gravity of the statement, but struggled to do so considering the nonchalance with which it rolled off her tongue.

'Don't get weird on me Ricky, it's okay. He spent more time on a corporate jet than he ever did with me. It's hard to mourn a father when I buried the idea of one about the same time I got my first period.'

'Still.' I said.

She shrugged, but didn't say anything.

'So you want me to hide out here?' I asked, trying to refocus the conversation.

'As good a place as any.'

'What about you? You staying here too?'

She smiled and shook her head. 'The cops are crawling all over Harlot's Den trying to pick up Big Dick. It'll look better if I'm just the girl that lives in the apartment above the bar and covers the odd shift.'

'As opposed to the girl that disappeared around the same time as Dick Sherman.'

'Correct. See you really are smarter than you look.'

'What the hell am I supposed to do, just sit around and sulk?'

She pointed to the laptop. 'I was thinking you'd get to work.'

'I thought we were shut down.'

She pointed again to the stats page for our site. I could see the numbers still climbing. 'That look like we should shut down? The way I see it, we're freed up to write about stuff that matters.'

'So we're what? Like, activists.'

'Nothing so dramatic. You're a smart guy. You know by now I've got somewhat of a network of like minded souls.'

'Souls or soldiers?'

'Kindred spirits.'

'And what do these kindred spirits want to report on?'

'The same as you and I.'

'What's that?'

'You tell me. What do you want to do? You can see the numbers there, we've got an audience.'

'I don't know. I mean, we've got a mass shooting on our hands. We could do a piece on that, kick start a gun control discussion.'

Veronica frowned and shook her head. 'Mainstream media's already picked it up. Plus, right now, it's a losing battle.'

'What do you mean? Mass shooting equals conversation on gun control. That's the formula as far as I can tell.'

'It's one that doesn't add up. When the people of this country decided it was acceptable for a gunman to kill twenty little kids in Connecticut, the debate ended.'

'You believe that?'

'I hope I'm wrong.'

'Me too. Anyway, what about terrorism? Terrorism is an audience winner isn't it?'

'I think we're at xenophobe saturation levels. Something will give sooner or later, but I don't think we'll move the dial today. You're thinking big, that's good I guess. Now think a little smaller. It's not always about taking big bites out of issues, sometimes its small, well-placed nibbles that create a reaction.'

I looked at her for a long time. She seemed more talkative, more alive than I'd seen her before. I felt a shift in her demeanor towards me, like we were bordering on partners now. But for the love of Christ she was being cryptic. 'Could you be slightly more vague?'

She smiled. 'Okay fine, but listen Ricky, you've heard all there is about mass shooting epidemics, terrorism, prescription drugs, etc. etc. Everyone else has as well. Tell the people something new, doesn't have to be huge, just thoughtful and a little different. Really think about it. If you have your pulpit. You've got your microphone and your attentive audience. What do you really want you say?'

I paused because I drew a blank. I knew the types of things I wanted to say. There were plenty. But when pushed, I couldn't name anything specific. From my entire pool of pent up lower middle class angst and hatred of all things that suck, I couldn't pull out one perfect, shiny, specific example. So I said the first thing that came to my mind. It turned out to be the truth. 'I just want to call bullshit on every trivial

fucking thing that's been stuffed down my throat for the last thirty years.'

Veronica stood up and put a hand on my shoulder. She smiled at me. 'See Ricky. Kindred spirits.' She held her hand to my cheek for a split second. It was the sweetest thing she's ever done to me and it was over in a fraction of a second. She took her hand away and walked over to the door.

'Wait, if I'm publishing stuff from here, won't the cops be able to track me down.'

She looked back at me. She frowned and blew air from her nose. I put my hands up. 'Sorry, forgot who I was dealing with. Where are you going?' I asked.

'You're not the only one with work to do.'

'What should I do in the meantime?'

She pointed at the laptop. 'Get online. Start researching. There's plenty out there for you to get started.' She walked off down the long hallway. I watched her for a few seconds. Then I got to work.

8

When I was little, we lived in a top floor apartment under a flight path. I'd lie awake at night frightened as I anticipated an airplane flying into our building and sending me into a blazing hell. That fear never did leave me. Eighteen years later I was in a barber's chair getting my haircut when I saw United 175 crash into the south tower. My barber was just as surprised as I was. About three thousand innocent people died that day. I walked around for two weeks with a bad haircut. Any other time in my life and that bad haircut would've really irked me.

My point is that a little perspective goes a long way. It can be both enlightening and debilitating. For me it's usually the latter. I've always had some major problems with perspective. For one, I could never keep it long term. Some people are built to be big thinkers dreaming beyond the day to day. I wish I could be that guy, but I'm just not. The weight of the day to day bullshit and minutia has been slowly burying me alive since my old man let on that Santa Clause was a fake. In fairness to Big Dick, he had to tell me. I was entering my teenage years and it was starting to get weird. He said it was for my own social benefit. He was probably right about that. So when Veronica told me to think a little smaller, I felt the shackles come off. Everyone wants to write the next big thing. The problem is that if you're waiting to figure out what that is before you put pen to paper, you're probably going to die of old age first.

I got to work right away, researching, making notes, scribbling down opening paragraphs to see if they led to any unlocking of ideas in my brain. It's a beautiful thing when you're doing something you enjoy, I mean when you're truly enthralled in something so that nothing else seems to distract or even exist except the here and now, the task at hand. There is no clock watching, no wandering thoughts, no dreams of vacations or other places, just full uninterrupted attention to what's in front of you at that moment. It happens so infrequently to me, but when I realize I'm in that moment I feel genuine joy to be alive. That feeling also has the opposite impact

of a long slow day's work. Instead of tired, when you finish up you're full of energy and smiles. Believe me, I was smiling like a delirious idiot when I hit the save button after what I thought was an insightful piece of work several hours later. I stood up and stretched in front of the large window that overlooked the garden. It had grown dark during my trance. Rain battered the glass and the overgrown trees danced in a violent wind. I struggled with the rusted lock on the window and managed to turn it just enough to get it opened. The wind drove droplets of rain into my face. I breathed in the moist air. I took the smell of wet grass and mud deep into my lungs and held it for a dozen seconds. The garden was severely overgrown, an unkempt facade masking its aristocratic potential. I cleared the rain from my face and looked out beyond the grounds of the estate. The house was still in the city, so its grounds were limited. The streetlights were sparse along the tree-lined road that ran behind the house. I peered into the dark street. I wasn't looking for anything specific, just wanted to clear my lungs of the old house's stale air. There were a few cars parked on the street. Mostly it was BMW's and Mercedes, maybe a scattered Audi every now and again. I scanned the road and paused when I saw a faint cloud

of smoke coming from a black Mercedes parked just beyond the garden's back wall. I looked closer. The car was definitely running, but I couldn't make out the shape of the body in the driver's seat. I put my hand on my forehead to shield a glare from a nearby street light, but it did nothing to improve my vision. Suddenly the car flashed its lights three times. I realized then that whoever it was could see me clearly, standing at the window of a lighted room in the dark. The driver must have guessed at my curiosity and he turned the interior lights on for a few seconds. His figure was clear for the moment, then it disappeared with the return to darkness. It was the same two gentlemen that dropped me at the house before. They were obviously instructed to stay close.

The realization that I was being watched was both creepy and unsurprising. I also felt some relief. For a loner, I really hated being by myself. I closed the window down and forced the rusty lock back into place. There was no curtain to close or blinds to pull. I walked out into the empty hallway. I tried a few doors until I found a bathroom. It appeared well stocked with toiletries and towels like you'd have it when expecting an overnight guest. There was a small linen closet inside the bathroom. I pulled a large

towel out and took it back to the room. I draped it over an empty curtain rod and stood back to assess the coverage. There were gaps on either side because of the extra wide window, but it gave some level of privacy at least. I sat back down at the desk in front of the laptop and unlocked the screen. I tried to read back what I'd just written, but not enough time had passed to be critical. The words just melted together on the page. My eyes weren't fresh in other words. I saved the work again and locked the screen as I stood up. It dawned on me that I hadn't eaten in quite some time. The hunger came on strong then and food was all I could think about it. I ventured back out into the giant hallway and followed the carpet out to the majestic staircase. I was guessing the house belonged to a Duke at some stage, maybe even a Sheikh in more recent times. I couldn't imagine any normal person casually occupying the premises, watching football and drinking beer on the Victorian furniture, getting up to take a leak and grab some Cheez Its at every commercial break. At the landing I wasn't sure where to turn for the kitchen, so I wandered. My steps echoed through the quiet house. I paused several times to be sure it was just my own steps causing the reverberation. I decided it was my steps only. The

accoutrements were my fear and imagination. I cursed the high ceilings and its acoustic properties. The house was mainly in darkness, but a glare from the moon provided some light thanks to the large windows. I eventually found the kitchen. It was more modern than I had expected. It was brighter than the rest of the house thanks to the moonlight reflected off of the stainless steel appliances. Everything looked new and unused, like a show house in a new development. I managed to locate the integrated refrigerator and opened it to review its contents. It was as well stocked as the upstairs bathroom. There were various juice containers, fresh milk, pre-packed sandwiches, beer and yogurts. It looked like someone went shopping for a single, lonely man. In other words, it was perfect. I took out a couple of the sandwiches and a bottle of some fruit juice concoction. There was a tall counter with stools in front. I took a seat at one and opened the first of the sandwiches. I had the first half of it shoved into my mouth before I noticed a notepad on the counter next to an old model mobile phone. I dragged it closer to me with my fingers. A fancy pen was rested on top of the pad. I lifted it off and held the weight of it in my hands. I could tell the handwriting on the note was

female before reading its contents. It was a patient script with flair and sharp lines. The text was brief. It mentioned the stocked fridge and bathroom, the location of the bedroom with clean sheets and a reminder to stay low lest I get picked up and coerced into giving a false confession of guilt by the fat O'Brien and the Blackpool Justice Department. The note's subtle lack of faith in my ability to hold strong under any scrutiny, intense or otherwise, was reminiscent of Big Dick. At the thought of my old man I felt a surge of both anger and sadness. By this time I could sense his latest betrayal would be his last and most impactful. I buried the pain of his cumulative rejection in a pile of turkey cold cuts with lettuce on white bread which I stuffed furiously into my gullet the way only an angry man eats. After the sandwiches were gone I relaxed a little. It must've been my blood sugar levelling off. I looked over the note again. It also contained a phone number to call should I need anything else. The number was followed by instructions to leave my own phone off and to use the one provided for all calls. I picked up the mobile on the counter. It looked ten years behind modern technology at least, but it switched on fine and appeared to get mobile service. I stuffed the phone and the note into my pocket and grabbed an apple from the counter. Enough time had passed and the food made me feel more alert, so I took the apple with me back through the mansion towards the room with the desk and laptop.

I settled back into the chair at my desk. Yes, by this stage I'd mentally assumed ownership of the house's contents. I nearly wanted to stencil my name on the mail box. Maybe not my own name since I was keeping low, but a clever alias like Paddy O'Furniture or Jack Goff. I was rejuvenated by the cold cuts and fruity concoction and the apple I was snapping bites from was delicious. I moved the cursor to awaken the screen and opened up the article I'd produced. With a focused pair of eyes and a cleared throat I began to real aloud. It was a trick Big Dick swore by, to be smoothly read aloud was to confirm the piece of work had good flow. I found the wording rolled easily off of my tongue, though the tone was a little dramatic for its less than life-altering content. I felt it was some of my better work on the whole. I'll paraphrase and change the names to protect the subject, but here's what it said more or less.

"Barry Burns is a modern day Robin Hood, an anti-establishment hero except you've never heard of him. I've heard it said that when it comes to corporations, the only thing that can kill off a behemoth is irrelevancy. 'Too big to fail' I'm sure you've heard that saying before. It's true unfortunately. Corporations over the years have acquired many rights that people have. Even today, they're lobbying for freedom from religious persecution. On the flip side, a corporation can weather corruption and outright criminality much better than any actual person. Barry Burns never went after any person. He was pushed by a corporation and when he was pushed too far, he pushed back. Maybe he didn't kill off a behemoth, but he took down a big one. Barry was like millions of us these days. He'd gone to college, he sacrificed, worked hard and performed well. He was rewarded with crippling student loans and by being stuffed into a grey cubicle with no windows. He was given an okay salary, just enough to make his monthly loan repayment, pay his rent and eat occasionally. Within just a few years, his bad posture from his poorly designed desk gave him back spasms and neck pain. Plus his eyes were definitely going from the hours on end staring at the computer screen. His downtrodden work environment didn't dampen his spirits however. His

effort was steady. His performance reviews were good, if not great. I know this because I've read them. For a while, everything was coming up Barry. Then the banks blew up the economy. Barry watched as colleagues that had grown into friends had their jobs axed one by one. It started slowly at first, but the pace accelerated quickly as the major shareholders pushed for securing profits. Before he knew it, Barry Burns had assumed the responsibilities of at least five colleagues. He was sinking quickly under that work load, but he couldn't raise his hand and complain for fear of being the next head on the chopping block. So he dug in and did what he could to stay afloat. He prioritized, stayed late, worked weekends, anything to keep up with the work load and hang onto his job. He was leaving late one spring night, the last one in the office as usual. He would make the rounds each night before heading off to switch off lights, power off coffee machines and photocopiers, things like that. He reached around to the back of a photocopier and switched the off button. When he straightened, he reached over and closed the lid to the copier. A sheet of paper flew out and slowly sailed to the ground. He did what any reasonable human would do. He bent over and picked it up. Next he read it. He did so with

the intention of deducing its owner and leaving it on the correct desk. Unfortunately for his company Barry Burns not only deduced its owner, but also understood its content. It was a note from one senior executive to another confirming the names of the individuals receiving their walking papers that very next day. There were five names on the list, but thanks to alphabetical placement, Barry Burns was listed first. Upon reading the note, Barry felt weak with betrayal. The stress and sweat he'd given to his beloved company, one that listed employee personal and professional growth and social responsibility as some of its core values, had all been for nothing. One way a corporation certainly can mimic an actual person is by engendering a feeling of betrayal in those that love it and trust it the most. Barry Burns became dizzy and disoriented. He walked back over to his desk and sat down. He kept all the lights off. He needed the darkness to shield his disappointment. He felt his lip quiver and tears form in his eyes, though none ever fell. He put his head down on his forearms and rubbed his eyes deep into the hairs along his wrists. Alas, Barry Burns does not stay down and out for long. He sniffed away his tears and sat up straight. His curious reflection stared back at him from the

empty monitor at his desk. He switched the computer back on and waited. An illustration of the circumstances in which fraud typically occurs includes a triangle with one word per side. They are opportunity, pressure and rationalization - check, check and check. That night was a hat trick for Barry Burns. He calmly pulled himself together and spent the next eight hours altering the company's supplier bank details to his own, raising large purchase orders to those same suppliers and doctoring up invoices to match those purchase orders. See, Barry Burns knew everything about everything. He'd put in the time, the hours upon hours pouring his soul into his work, absorbing others' jobs out of necessity and without reward or recognition. Most importantly, he knew a payment run was going out that very next day. It was a Wednesday. Payments went out every Wednesday.

The next morning no one noticed that Barry Burns wore the same shirt and tie as the previous day. He'd put in such long hours and dealt with constant pressure and demand that he always looked haggard. This Wednesday was no different. He was often the first man in and the last to leave. There was nothing out of place. Nothing out of the ordinary. It was just Barry being Barry. At ten in the morning, he was

called into the CFO's office. The last remaining human resources person sat at the table in the office. She looked as worn out as Barry Burns did, the toll of handing out pink slips slowly chewing away at a fragile soul. A security guard stood just outside the office door. Barry Burns was handed a folder and a white envelope which he assumed was his final paycheck. He couldn't recall the words spoken. It didn't matter. They were empty and rehearsed. The speech he imagined was the same one delivered over a hundred times at this stage, maybe even a thousand.

Barry took his white envelope and new beginnings folder and walked out. He went directly to his bank and inquired about wire transfers, restrictions, and withdrawal limits, among a hundred other topics. Within twenty four hours he was over three million dollars richer than before. He moved the funds immediately and continuously for the next seven days, withdrawing as much as possible in cash within that same timeframe. Then Barry Burns disappeared. To this day, no one has seen him. He was married to the job, no wife, no girlfriend, and no kids. His mother died of cancer years before, his father succumbed to a broken heart shortly thereafter. Barry Burns is a ghost and God willing he'll remain

that way.

The kicker is that his company never had a clue. It took at least thirty more days for complaints from suppliers to even register. It got to a stage that several key suppliers cut the company off. Business stopped. Then the panic struck. They needed to be paid. So guess what? The company tried to pay them, hundreds of them. Imagine that. Guess where that round of payments went? Millions of dollars? You guessed right. It landed in the bank accounts listed for those suppliers on their system, one belonging to a man by the name of Barry Burns. It was dispersed into thin air shortly thereafter. Suppliers pulled out, filed lawsuits, went public, investigations ensued, disclosures, et cetera et cetera. The share price plummeted. Major shareholders lost millions upon millions. Finally, the company folded. All this happened courtesy of Barry Burns, or as I think of him, Robin Hood."

I saved the article for the hundredth time. I stood up and put my hands on the back of the chair and crouched down into a stretch. I liked what I had written. I liked the story, the main character, and the fact the guy got the last laugh on a heartless corporation that blindly paved the way to its own

demise. I liked how the wealthy shareholders were left scratching their heads and pulling out bunny ears from their pockets. It wasn't earth shattering content, nor was it meant to be. But I wrote it, I enjoyed doing so and god damn it I stood up straight, then reached over to the mouse and I clicked on 'publish'.

9

I stared up at the elaborate ceiling in the spare bedroom. The design made me feel like I was sleeping in a fancy hotel lobby. The room was as drafty as one too. I couldn't sleep. I kept my eyes shut for a while in an attempt to do so, but I gave up as dawn broke. There were too many thoughts running through my head. I worried about the job I'd never returned to. It wasn't so much the question of whether I'd ever be paid to work again, it was more that I could've sworn I'd left something behind in my desk drawer, but I couldn't remember what it was. It was probably just in my head. The only thing I ever kept there was hair wax and emergency ties. Then I thought about how emergency ties were like the backup quarterback of your professional wardrobe. They weren't the best you have, but they damn sure better be decent. Next I thought about Veronica for a little while. She was still a mystery to me, but the longer I knew her, the more I was developing a picture of who the girl really was, young, hurt, and angry. On second thought it wasn't exactly an in depth analysis. Although I had learned she was a secret heiress to a vacant mansion in the right part of town and that she was a well-connected organizer of something, though I couldn't tell what exactly. Mostly though, my time awake was occupied with Big Dick. I felt used and betrayed. For over thirty years I had felt a longing and pure neglect. I'm not sure which was worse. More than anything however, I was embarrassed for myself. A lifetime of neglect that I swept under the carpet at a moment's notice just to gain favor with the old man. I should've known something was off when he called me in to see him. I could've asked questions, thought critically about what he said to me, I could've done all those things. All of which were pure characteristics of good journalism, something that should come naturally to anyone with journalistic talents. I'd done none of that. Instead I blindly believed the slimy bastard. I thought back to his face and his demeanor the last time I saw him. It was like my pain, my three decades of

cumulative heartache didn't even register with him. At that moment I hated him, or at least I told myself I did. I wanted to and wished that I could.

When the sun came up it burned through the closed curtains in the bedroom. The room warmed up quickly once it did. I was exhausted, but I felt I should get up. For a while I continued to lay there. My legs ached. It was my calves especially. I knew it was from my escape down the long flight of stairs the day before. My body wasn't used to exercise. I also had to pee. It was bordering on urgent. I still refused to get up.

I had just about convinced my legs to move when I heard a door creak. I nearly pissed myself with surprise. I chanced a peek towards the door. Veronica stood in the doorway with her hands on her slim hips. I felt sudden excitement. I tried to say hello, but it came out as a croak. I cleared my throat and tried again. She walked into the room and over to the window nearest the bed. I could smell her perfume or shampoo. It was fragrant and delicious whatever it was. She grabbed the curtains and pulled them open. The room went bright with sunlight. I threw my hands over my eyes to shield them. It was a vampire's reaction to daylight. She walked around the bed to the

other side of the room and did the same to the second window. I managed a much less dramatic reaction this time. 'The moment's past.' I thought.

She sat down in a chair in front of a makeup mirror in the corner of the room. I sat up in the bed, careful to keep the covers close to me. I would've done some pushups or something if I knew she was going to be giving me a wakeup call. 'I wasn't expecting you.' I said.

'It doesn't smell great in here.' She said.

'Oh.' I thought about crawling back under the covers and suffocating myself.

She noticed my embarrassment and smiled. 'Smells like dude. Why don't you go shower and then meet me in the kitchen?'

I nodded, then said 'Wait. I don't have a change of clothes.'

'It's taken care of.' She said.

'Of course it is.' I thought.

'I hung up some stuff in the closet in the bathroom. It should last you a week or two at least.'

'You went by my place?'

She shook her head. 'No, I had someone run to the mall and just buy whatever the mannequin was wearing.'

'Thanks.' I said.

'Meet me downstairs in the kitchen.' She said. She got up and left the room.

I waited a few seconds until I heard her footsteps on the stairs. I was still being bashful. The water pressure in the shower was better than any apartment I ever had. It was like standing under a waterfall only warmer. I still maintain I've never been cleaner than after that five minute rinse. The clothes she had procured for me were also much better than anything I owned for myself, meaning across the board, the style, quality and fit. I walked into the kitchen with an air of confidence and swagger that I normally kept in reserve until after a half-bottle of whiskey. Veronica was leaning on the counter looking into a laptop with a coffee mug in her hand. When she heard me enter she looked up. I noticed her head tilt a little first before she smiled. I saw the pot of coffee and poured myself a cup before taking the stool across from her. I took a sip from the mug. 'Good coffee.' I said. It was true. It was damn good coffee in fact. She probably had a bean guy. She didn't respond, just kept her eyes on me. 'What?' I asked.

'Nothing. Just, you almost look like an adult.'

'Thanks. The mannequin had good taste. So,

what's going on? Have you heard anything?'

'I worked a shift at the Den last night. As expected there were cops around asking questions.'

'Questions of you?'

'Yes. Of me and everyone else in there, of which there weren't many.'

'They ask about me?'

She nodded. 'You and Big Dick, whereabouts, last seen, the usual.'

'Did they say I was a suspect?'

'No, but they wouldn't if you were. It's the same as you'd expect, just looking to talk, worried about your safety, things like that.'

'Bullshit in other words.'

'Yes very much so.'

'Was O'Brien there himself?'

'I didn't see him. He's not a detective is he?'

'Honestly I don't know what he is. He's a curious son of a bitch regardless.'

She reached over to the edge of the counter and slid a brown paper bag in my direction. 'Bagels.' She said.

'Thanks.' I reached in and grabbed one. They were warm and still soft. I thought about the house, the clothes, the food. 'Do I owe you for all this?' I mean. Are you going stick me with an invoice that I can't pay at the end of this?'

She smiled. 'Where do you think this all ends Ricky?'

It was a basic question and unsurprisingly one I'd never really considered. I didn't bother guessing.

'Just keep producing like you have been and we'll call it even. Consider it your paycheck.'

I thought about it. I'd never afford that house or clothes, or the gourmet bagels on one of my paychecks. Still, I relented. 'I wrote one last night. Published it, but it was late. I haven't checked the stats yet.'

'They're good.' She said. 'Why do you think I'm here?'

'You liked the article?'

'I didn't say that, but now that you mention it, yes. I did.'

'Great.'

'Well, good.'

'Okay, I'll take good.'

'I like what you did putting it into a narrative. It reads more like a piece of fiction than a news article.'

'Oh yeah?'

'Which is it, fiction or news?'

I was offended. My journalistic integrity questioned again. Then I remembered there was a pattern there, so my defensiveness eroded as quickly as it arrived. 'It's news. At least, I think it's news. I came across it doing some research online last night.'

'Good. Either way. It doesn't really matter.'

'It doesn't?'

'Not really, no.'

I was too tired to bother asking. 'Fine, okay.'

'Good. Anyway, I liked your underdog story. Everybody likes to hear about the little guy coming out on top. It was clever, especially painting the big bad corporation as the villain.'

'Thanks, I felt it's topical these days.'

'It's been topical since the industrial revolution.' She said. She walked over to the sink and poured the dregs of her coffee down the drain. 'It's the right theme.' She said. 'See if you can put out a few more like that, at least while you're here and you have the opportunity.' She opened the dishwasher door that I hadn't noticed existed. She put the cup in the top tray face down and slammed it shut. 'As for me, I have to go see some people. I'll check in later with you. Let you know if I hear anything else or run into your friend O'Brien.'

'Speaking of people. I noticed my babysitters last night.'

'I heard.'

'Should I expect to see them around?'

'They'll be around, whether or not you see them.'

'That's necessary?'

'What was the line the cops said? Worried about your personal safety?'

I laughed, but not on the inside.

'Bye for now Ricky.' She said.

'Bye for now.'

I took out another bagel and bit into it. They really were spectacular. When Veronica left, I wandered around the downstairs for a while until I grew bored. Eventually, I think around early afternoon, I settled back at my desk and got to work. By that time, I was already into a rhythm.

That rhythm carried over for a few days then into the following week. I'd get up, shower, drink fresh juice, and eat gorgeous bagels. Then I'd start researching after lunch. An idea would form just before dinner. A first draft would be nailed down before dusk. Finally, the completed product would be finished and out to the world by midnight. Next I'd stare at the ceiling until dawn. Then repeat. There was no one there to bother me, no asshole boss looking over my shoulder, no awkward lunch room conversations, I was free. Well, actually I wasn't free at all, I was trapped, but damn it, at the beginning I felt free. I enjoyed researching and I loved writing. So not every article I wrote was gold, so what. I have to say there were at least a few good ones.

I started with a light-hearted piece. It was an homage to a former corporate lawyer who had a nervous breakdown after he lost his job in the downturn. He couldn't practice law anymore and no company would hire him, so he resorted to spending his days drafting legal letters and sending them out to companies threatening to file a lawsuit for one reason or another. He started out sending one or two a day, basically anytime he received some unsolicited marketing email or text message he'd get fed up and shoot a letter off. He found that companies seemed ready to settle for cash quickly instead of chancing a costly civil suit. He started getting random checks in the mail, so he was inspired to up the stakes. Now he writes up to a thousand letters a week. He has about a ten percent response rate and clears about five grand a week. It's a glorious success story.

Later in the week I put together a nice narrative

on a pair of cousins that worked together at a software company. Let's call them Bill and Bob. Bob was a hotshot programmer. He developed a lot of the code the company's main product was designed with until he was forced out of the organization. The CEO felt he got as much as he needed from Bob. He felt Bob had gained too much power and influence. So he canned him and his entire team. Bill stuck around on a different team. In defense of his family name he struck back by blowing the whistle on some accounting irregularities he'd come across, which he otherwise would've ignored. The SEC swooped in and tore the place apart. They uncovered a boat load of fraud and corruption. For Bill's assistance, the government gave him a check for thirty percent of the total fine imposed on the company, which was in the millions. The board of directors ousted the CEO, CFO and most of senior management. They called Bob and asked him back. Bob told them to eat shit. Bill used half of the reward check to start up a competitor company with Bob. He used the remaining cash to pay a group of hackers to launch cyber attacks on their former company and several other large competitors. They referred to it as due diligence. While those companies suffered, Bill and

Bob LLC gained massive market share, won several entrepreneurial awards, took their company public, completed a hostile takeover of their former company, ousted the board and the remaining senior management team then reinstated Bob's team at the head of the organization. It was poetry.

My favorite piece by far however, was a little story I put together on good old Bud Kershaw. With a name like Bud, you'd expect the man to be from Texas or at least somewhere down there. Bud sure did live in Texas and he spoke with a drawl and he wore boots and a big fucking hat. However Bud was actually from Connecticut, somewhere close to the New York border, a born and bred Yankee, though he'd never let on that was the case. Bud was President of a company called Just Short Loans. Just Short Loans is what you'd call politely a payday loan company. A little less polite reference would be a predatory lender, which is exactly what they were. You don't get to the top of one of those companies without getting blood on your hands and Bud's hands were red with it, know that from the outset. The problem however was that Bud got rich, then he very quickly got greedy and bored. First it was the horses, then football, then anything to do with NCAA, didn't

matter what. He was dead broke before he even got to play cards. Down and out, but with his reputation still intact he took the back door to get some cash. He took a loan from a street guy to pay down the bookies so he could avoid some broken fingers and toes. So he paid the bookies, but then he couldn't pay the loan sharks. It was lose an eye or come clean. So he came clean and took a loan from Just Short to get the sharks off his back. What he didn't figure was that his own company would treat him like any other name in the book. Just Short took his house, his car, his ski lodge, his boat. His wife left him, his kids disowned him, and his mother died of a heart attack from the embarrassment. He still couldn't pay the fees. When there was nothing to take, they took him to court. His bookie agreed to drive him, but he never showed on the day. He got slapped with contempt for missing his court date. He couldn't pay the fine, so they gave him a night in jail. In the prison, he was recognized by a man that got popped for robbing a gas station. The man was robbing a gas station because Just Short Loans had taken his house and threatened to take his ex-wife's house because he had co-signed for her. If that happened, he was going to lose visitation rights with his kids. He couldn't find work. He was starved

and desperate. So he tried to rob a gas station. He failed. He was tossed in prison. He saw Bud. He snapped. Bud was a big man. He fought back and won. The man never got up. Now Bud's doing twenty-five to life in some dust bowl near the Mexican border. Bud didn't understand karma. He probably did afterwards. You got to love karma, don't you?

10

Are you the kind of person that gets sick of a vacation by the end of it? I definitely am, I can assure you of that. I hate that about myself, but I can't seem to change. I've heard time and again that you can never have too much of a good thing. I'm the guy that would beg to differ. If you have too much of a good thing, it loses its appeal. In other words, it becomes ordinary. I truly hope there are many of you out there disagreeing with me right now, but I'm not so sure. I loved getting up every day, enjoying breakfast, relaxing until lunch, and writing until dark. I loved it, that is, until I didn't. Realistically that took thirteen days. It wasn't even a full two weeks. Thirteen days, one story per day. That's thirteen articles to go with the others I'd produced before Big Dick organized the mass murder of innocent people out for a stroll on

the boardwalk. It doesn't sound like such a long time, but after the first few days it began to wear on me. Plus it wasn't like Veronica was stopping by every day to hang out. She popped in a handful of times, brought food, clean clothes, some news of the outside world, but not much else. She never stayed long. She was always on her way out to meet a mysterious someone about something. She's not one to elaborate on details, at least not with me. My babysitters, as I called them, they stuck around, but it was always at a distance. I never had so much as a chat with those guys again. So I had to face facts. I was lonely and needed some human contact. Do you understand how conflicting it is for an anti-social man such as myself to need to be around people? I don't get it, but that's how I felt. I needed to be around people. It didn't matter who really. I'd heard very little else on the cops or their investigation or Big Dick. In my mind, I'd moved on. I assumed everyone else had as well.

I saw out the window that the Mercedes was parked in its usual spot. I thought for a minute about whether I'd be able to simply slip out the front door. Recent history pointed to that being way too easy. I guessed that my babysitters in the Mercedes likely had a video feed of all the major entrance and exit

points to the house and grounds. I never did find out if I was right, but I assume I was. I needed a distraction, just something to get these guys to take their eye off the ball for a few seconds. I thought about what Big Dick might do, he was probably better at improvisation than I'd ever be. Although, he'd probably have paid his fixer to pop the two guys or something like that. That was extreme. As far as I could tell they were on my side, at least that was my take on it. I just needed to get out of that house for a minute, feel part of society, and feel normal. I thought about it some more and decided on a more practical solution, something more Eddie Murphy than Big Dick. I ordered a pizza. I had to call it in to explain the whole deliver to the car, not a house thing, but I made it work. I shut down Veronica's phone afterwards and stuck it in the draw. I stuck my own phone in my pocket, but kept it turned off for now. I stayed at the laptop pretending to tinker away at some research, while keeping a peripheral eye on the Mercedes out the window. Half an hour later, I saw an old Ford escort pull up in front of the Mercedes. I moved right away. I slammed down the laptop and raced down the stairs. I probably could have used the front door then, there wasn't an alarm that I was

aware of, but I went out a side window anyway, it felt right. The drop to the grass below was much longer than I'd considered. The shock of the ground hurt my heels and I went down on a knee briefly. I jumped to my feet and ran to the far wall. It wasn't very high, but I had to fight my way through overgrown bushes to reach it. I made it up and over within twenty seconds. The drop down to the side walk wasn't as far, but it still hurt when I landed. I didn't look back towards the house. I jogged for about a block, then slowed to a brisk walk. The estate was in an upscale part of the city. The trees lined both sides of the street and were in full bloom, so I was afforded some natural cover as I walked away. I made it to a large intersection. I pushed the walk button and waited for the line of cars to stop. Out of the house, my cocoon for the last near two weeks, and now beyond the natural tree cover, I felt exposed as I waited at the cross walk. I hadn't taken a hat with me and the warm weather didn't justify a popped collar. I grew nervous waiting and decided to keep moving. I ditched the large intersection and turned up another street that led up to the river that divided Blackpool's north and south parts of the city. Harlot's Den was just past the river on the north side. I was only a half mile south of the

river on the same longitude line. The proximity made me anxious. There could still be eyes on the Den. I was regretting my decision to leave the grounds of Veronica's estate more with each passing second. I paused and stared ahead. I could already see the bridge in the distance for the trains to cross the river. I was considering turning back when I saw a white car turn onto the road from a side street and start driving towards me. I could see the shape of the sirens on the hood. 'Shit.' I thought. I didn't want to rouse suspicion, so I pulled out my phone and stared at the blank screen then started walking forward again. The cop car was about twenty yards away when I ducked into a small supermarket for cover. I walked around the shop for a minute pretending to search for something. A young guy in an apron walked by me and asked if I needed help with anything. I brushed him off with something like, 'I'm all set.' A second later I realized I had zero money on me. I had a debit and credit card, but I thought if the cops were out looking for me there might be a trace on them. I remembered my phone in my pocket. I pulled it out to double check it was still off, which it was. I needed to keep it that way. If they could've got me on GPS while the phone was off, I'd already be in custody. I'm surprised Veronica didn't object to me keeping the phone in the house. She probably had a tech guy that could jam the signal or something James Bond like that. I walked down an aisle that had newspapers and magazines stacked on the shelf and piled at the floor in front of it. I picked up a magazine and flicked through it. I pretended to read the headlines, just a frugal man considering whether to buy *Good Housekeeping* or *Sluts and Butts.* The man in the apron walked by the aisle and looked down at me. He paused for a moment then nodded and got back to work. I felt I had exhausted my welcome and it was either time to buy something, which I couldn't do, or time to leave. I reached over and placed the magazine I was holding neatly back into its spot on the shelf.

I was about to leave, but then something caught my eye. I wasn't sure why it did, there was no obvious reason that it should have grabbed my attention. There in the top right hand corner of the daily paper was a column heading in bold type. It was the *Blackpool Times*, the only serious daily title remaining after the *Blackpool Daily* sunk. It read 'Who is this Blackpool Prophet, really?' It referenced an article on page five. I quickly leafed through the pages and scanned page five with eyes darting around

like a coke head watching a tennis match. I found the article midway down the page, a slim column with text only, no advertising clouding the layout. The article talked about a recent spike in corporate fraud cases and a jump in the number of whistle blower disclosures resulting in major investigations. It referenced a major cyber attack and loss of customer data of a fast growing software company, the very one with award winning entrepreneurs Bill and Bob at the head. The cyber attack wiped out the company's share price. Bill and Bob lost millions, maybe a billion and the board of directors were said to be planning a coup to oust Bill and Bob from the organization. The article moved on to outline the investigation launched by the FBI on the Just Short Loan company and several other payday loan organizations operating across several states in the U.S. At last it included a description of the mysterious and violent execution of one Robert 'Bud' Kershaw while in custody at some medium security prison in a remote Texas county. When I read this last part, I thought about Bud Kershaw meeting his end at the tapping of my fingertips. The hairs on the back of my neck stood up. I rubbed my forehead and dragged my hand over my eyes. I finished the last paragraph. There were no

names given. There was however a mention of a potential link with the shooting weeks earlier on the riverfront in Blackpool. That case remained noticeably unsolved and the media felt potentially under-investigated.

When I finished reading I felt nauseous. I closed the newspaper and stuffed it back into the rack. I put my hands on my knees to stop myself from falling over. Everything went blurry. I saw a pair of sneakers walk towards me and saw the hang of an apron at the man's knees. I think he asked if I was all right. He reached out to hold me up, but I pushed his hand away and stumbled to the end of the aisle, then over through the sliding doors. Outside the light was a blinding white. I managed to put my back against the wall of the shop and slide to a sitting position. I leaned back further against the wall and tried to get ahold of my breathing. I couldn't. There were short breaths that got faster and faster, but took less and less air into my lungs. I laid down on the ground and kept my knees up. Slowly I felt the tightness in my chest start to ease. The blinding light eased into normal daylight and everything stopped spinning. I regained control of my breathing and a minute later everything seemed to return to normal. I had a bad

headache, but that was it. I became acutely aware that I was causing a scene while trying to maintain a low profile. I noticed the man from the shop standing next to me. I glanced up past his apron to his face. He was nodding. 'Shit' I thought. I sat up quickly.

'Don't worry.' The man said. 'I called you an ambulance. It'll be here any second.' He crouched down to be eye level with me and put his hand on my shoulder. He must have registered my sudden pupil dilation and slowly took his hand away. He seemed intent on touching me for some reason.

'I'm fine.' I said. I got up quickly. I was little lightheaded when I stood, but it didn't last.

He said. 'Don't know man, think you should . . .'

'I'm fine.' I cut him off. I looked up and down the street. There was no sign of the cop car that had caused me to turn into the shop initially. I took a step to leave. The man tried to hold me back.

'Listen.' He said.

'You listen.' I said. I stared at him for a second, then softened my voice a little. 'Thanks. But, I'm leaving. I'm fine buddy. You can have a clear conscience.' He considered my response. I was preparing to get by him with force. He looked sturdy. I'd have to go dirty from the outset. I contemplated a

kick to the balls or a poke to the eye. I decided on the eye. He could block a kick and I might stub my toe on his shin. Although the stubbed toe anger is superhuman and I thought it might work to my advantage. It didn't come to any of that. The man said. 'Good luck then buddy.' And he went back into his shop.

I took off in a brisk walk up the street. I quickly made some twists and turns. If a cop responded to the call before an ambulance, the man from the shop would no doubt give a description that might match someone they're looking for. I needed to be out of sight. I needed to think, but there wasn't time. What I'd read was really beginning to register. Something was up, but I didn't know what. Everything I wrote about was being used as bait, or guidance, some kind of message. There was only one person that could explain it. I had to make it to Veronica's apartment without being picked up. I knew there'd be cops staking out Harlot's Den, but I needed to chance it. I crossed the river over the crowded foot bridge. I kept my face down and walked swiftly through the crowd. I was still well dressed thanks to my borrowed wardrobe. I could've been any office worker walking back from coffee break or lunch. I figured if the cops

were watching Harlot's Den, it would have to be within a line of sight to the main entrance. As far as I knew there was no reason for them to suspect the girl that lived next door and therefore no need to have eyes on the fire escape in the back of her apartment.

I took an indirect route to avoid any likely stakeout points. I slid through the depths of Blackpool's inner city alleyways, each one more grotesque than the last. I stood under a ripped awning outside the backdoor to a Chinese restaurant. I could smell the fatty grease from the kitchen and felt the slick runoff under my shoes thanks to a nearby drain. I waited close to a minute for any activity in the back alley. I could see Veronica's fire escape. With my eyes, I followed the steel steps up to her bedroom window. It didn't look open, but I suspected it was still unlocked. I didn't have a plan beyond getting into her apartment. I needed to talk to her, to have her explain to me what was going on. I needed to understand. I knew I was taking a risk breaking into her apartment. That was obvious. For one, it's a crime, but much worse than that, I was concerned how she'd react to being surprised. I had visions of looking cross-eyed at a ninja star stuck into my forehead. At that moment, it didn't matter. I believed

I had to get off the street immediately. I surveyed the alley one last time, then I breathed in one last deep mouthful of greasy dumpster grime and took off towards Veronica's back entrance. As I approached the fire escape, I realized the ladder was too high to reach without jumping. I had to back up against the far wall for leverage. I took off in a run and jumped with my hands outstretched. I missed the first time. I wasn't known for my vertical prowess. I felt like a fat kid on the basketball court trying to slap the backboard. I looked around worried someone might happen upon my idiocy and catch me on video. I could never decide whether internet shaming had more in common with the Salem Witch trials or the French Revolution. Probably the latter, it's all fun and games until it's your neck waiting on the guillotine. If Jesus were alive today, he might phrase it something like 'Let he who has never been a dick cast the first tweet.' I think it was the fear of being an internet sensation as a dunce criminal that gave me the extra inch I needed. I grabbed the rung with both hands and held on for dear life. I swung back and forth a couple of times from the momentum. Slowly then I started to pull myself up. I felt the scrape of metal on metal and braced myself as the ladder slammed down

another foot. I continued climbing. Once my foot caught the bottom rung I was up in seconds. I climbed to the first landing and continued on. A couple of seconds later I was outside of Veronica's bedroom. The curtains were pulled, but there was a gap, which I was able to peak through. The bedroom was dark, but I could see through the door to the kitchen. I couldn't see much else, but I could tell a light was on. I thought about my next move. I should've been inside already, but manners got the best of me. I decided to knock. I rapped on the window gently. One does not knock aggressively on another's bedroom window or so I thought at the time as if it mattered. I didn't wait long after that. I couldn't see anyone moving to let me in. It was thirty seconds at most. I put my hands against the glass and pushed slightly to get them to stick. Then I slowly slid them upwards. As I had guessed, the window was unlocked. It lifted with a little hassle. It was an old window that creaked when raised. I managed to open it enough with my palms to slide a hand underneath. I pushed it open the full way and reached in to spread the curtains. I stepped inside, trying my best not to break anything. I thought I succeeded until I brought my other leg around and knocked a framed picture off

the bedside table. I picked it up and looked at it. It was an old photo of a young girl and her parents. Veronica looked different as a child, though her hair had the same frizz. Her mother looked like an eighties version of what Veronica looked like now. Her dad looked older and wasn't what I expected. His face was round and he was balding. He wore a big grin and had his long arms around both the woman and the child. I checked the frame and was relieved that the glass hadn't broken. I placed it up-right back where it was next to the bed. I slowly walked over to the doorway. I paused and listened out for any movement. I thought I could hear a murmur of a television on low volume. I stood at the doorway and called out. 'Veronica?' I stayed in the same spot waiting on a response. A few seconds past and nothing. I stepped into the kitchen. I looked around the room. It looked different from the last time I walked through it. It dawned on me the difference was that the room was a mess. There were dirty dishes in the sink and empty cups on the counter. There were empty beer bottles stacked on the counter up against the refrigerator. I walked over to them. I could smell the stale beer from the bottles' remnants. I walked over to the sink. It felt all wrong. I didn't

know her well or very long for that matter, but this mess didn't feel like Veronica's. I stood considering what this meant. Did she have a boyfriend after all? Or a roommate I wasn't aware of? I heard a cough from the other room and froze. It was a man's cough. Deep and heavy with phlegm. I almost gagged listening to it. The weird thing was that the disgusting hack sounded familiar. I thought about that sound for a minute and considered why I knew it. It dawned on me the same moment I noticed the empty bottles of fireball whiskey piled next to the garbage bin.

As soon as I realized it was Big Dick I could smell him. His scent hadn't changed since I was a child, even before his cinnamon whiskey days. I started walking towards the room. I picked up an empty fireball bottle on my way. I felt its weight in my hand. I knew it could do damage if it came to that. I didn't know why Big Dick was in Veronica's apartment. The only ideas that peppered my brain were the sick, revolting ones. I crept into the room. From behind, I could see his old hat sitting on the top of his head. The weight of his neck dented the top cushion of the armchair. He hadn't heard me call out earlier and he didn't seem to notice me approach. I

walked around the chair. He looked like a fat corpse in an old blanket. His eyes were shut. If I hadn't heard him cough before, I'd have guessed he was dead. He'd probably smell the same. I stood between him and the television. I could feel my heart beating in my chest. I watched his heavy chest move slowly up and down. My anger was growing with each second. I gripped the neck of the whiskey bottle so tight that my knuckles were translucent. 'Dick.' I said. My voice came out older and deeper than it typically did. The bass of it seemed to linger around the room of the quiet apartment. Big Dick twitched his head. He slowly moved a hand up to his face. I watched the big paw rub the drool from the side of this mouth. I was about to say something else, but I heard a toilet flush and heard a door creak open, then slam shut. The noise caught me off guard. I looked out towards the kitchen. My eyes darted around until the shape of a man filled the doorway. He paused at the entrance and looked me up and down. His eyes hung onto the bottle in my hand. I looked down at it, then back at Big Dick. When I did, his eyes were opened and he gave me a large grin. He brought his boot up and kicked the glass bottle out of my hand. It went airborne then smashed against the far wall and

landed in several pieces. I looked at the mess, then back over at the man in the doorway. I recognized him as a man I'd run into before picking up Veronica at her place a couple weeks ago. He shook his head at me and then walked over to the broken glass. He was sweeping the pieces into a pile with his foot. Big Dick was laughing at the mess he made.

I looked down at him. He made no effort to get up. 'Why the hell are you laughing?'

'You really gonna hit your old man with that bottle? I didn't think you'd have the balls.'

'I wasn't going to hit anyone with anything. I didn't know what I was walking into. What the hell are you doing here anyhow?'

The man cleaning up the glass shushed the two of us. 'These walls are paper thin.' He whispered. The cops are crawling all over this place and you two are drawing attention to yourselves. No wonder Veronica wanted you both kept under lock and key.'

I looked over at the man then back at Big Dick. Dick didn't say anything, but he lifted up his hand, which was previously covered with a blanket. A handcuff was stretched across his wrist. It barely fit, but he was locked in. There was a chain linked to it a couple of feet long. The far end was hooked into a

radiator up against the wall. Just then I heard a noise in the hallway. It sounded like footsteps. Big Dick and I froze. The man cleaning up stopped mid sweep and listened. There were muffled voices. They sounded angry. I heard the shake of keys and then a latch unlock before the door opened. When it did, the voices stopped. The footsteps didn't. Seconds later, the living room became very small once Veronica walked in book-ended by my babysitters. I gave them each a head nod when we made eye contact, the international sign language for what's up. For two well-dressed and confident grown men, they looked like a couple of dogs that shit on the carpet and got their noses forced into it. Veronica looked irritated and unsurprised.

'We didn't save you any pizza.' The taller man said.

'How was it?' I asked. 'Any good?'

'Decent. I prefer pepperoni though.'

'I'll keep it in mind for next time.' I said.

Veronica cut us both off. 'Ricky, we should talk.' She said. I looked at her, then around at the others in the room. I wanted to have a conversation definitely, but not with a panel. I looked at Big Dick. 'Fine.' I said. 'But first, you want to explain this?' I asked pointing at him.

'What did he tell you already?'

'He hasn't told me anything. I've only been here a minute.'

She pointed at the dent in the wall and the shattered glass on the floor. 'Long enough to raise hell I see.'

'It was him.' I said pointing at Big Dick.

She shook her head. 'Why don't you tell him Dick? Tell him why you're here.'

'Bollocks to both of you.' Big Dick said. He pulled at the cuff and chain around his wrist. 'I'll do my talking when you remove my jewelry. Veronica didn't respond to him. She looked back to me. She looked very tired. The bags under her eyes added several years to her appearance.

'Why does he even talk like that?' She asked.

'He spent time in Ireland reporting on the Troubles. When he came back he apparently couldn't put a sentence together without saying bollocks or shite.'

She smiled. When she did some of my anger receded. My questions remained however. She sensed that. The man that swept up the broken glass spoke up. 'I found him.' He said. 'He was shit-faced, stumbling his way towards Harlot's Den.'

'The cops missed him?'

'Just.' Veronica said.

The man continued. 'I went to the store a few blocks away. He was lucky. I grabbed him and took him up the fire escape before anyone saw him.'

I was thinking about my own excursion a few minutes before. 'It wasn't easy.' The man said.

Veronica said. 'Dick's number one on the cops' list of people of interest. In other words, he's a suspect in the shooting.'

I nodded my head. 'You're number two on their list.' She said to me. I felt guilty all of a sudden, like I'd broken curfew. Veronica's voice had a 'not mad, just disappointed' tone to it. I almost fell for her act again, but I steeled myself.

'You should've let him get picked up.' I said. The room went silent. Even Big Dick's heavy breathing quieted. 'What?' I said. 'He is fucking guilty. He told me so himself.'

'Listen you little bollocks, I never told the guy to start firing off rounds at pedestrians.' Big Dick said.

'I don't think anyone gives a shit what you meant to do or not. He was your guy right? Your fixer?'

'You little fucker.' He said.

Veronica interrupted us both. 'Enough.' She said. She turned to me. 'Ricky, how do you think this plays out if O'Brien and the cops get their hands on Big Dick?'

I shrugged my shoulders. I was trying for casual indifference.

'He'll take you down with him if he can.' She said. I looked over at Big Dick. He stared blankly at me. He didn't disagree. I knew she was right.

'And you too no doubt.' I said. She nodded in agreement.

'That's why he's here. For our safety, not his.' She paused. 'So, what do you want me to do with him?'

I thought about it some more. If O'Brien picked up Big Dick, which he would, he'd tie him to this shooting and probably a few more things. He had too, Big Dick was nothing if not sloppy. I knew now he'd try to take me or anyone else he could down with him. But honestly at that moment, I just didn't give a shit. I just wanted the old man out of my face so I could get to the bottom of things with Veronica. 'Cut him loose.' I said. 'He's a big man, I'm sure he can take care of himself.'

Veronica looked over at the man next to the pile

of broken glass. 'You heard him.' She said. 'Get him out of here.'

'You're sure?' The man asked. Veronica looked back to me and I nodded.

'You heard Ricky.' She said.

The man dug into his pocket and pulled out a tiny silver key. He reached out and grabbed Big Dick's forearm. Big Dick let him work without interruption. The cuff fell to the ground as soon as the man turned the key. It was propelled by Big Dick's enormous wrist that expanded as the metal gave way. It must have been hanging on by a single rung. Big Dick rubbed his newly freed wrist and slowly got to his feet.

'Can you go out the back at least?' Veronica asked. 'I saw an unmarked car at the end of the block.'

'I'll help him.' "The man with the cuffs said.

Veronica turned to the others. 'He'll need a hand down.' She said. Both men nodded and followed Big Dick out of the room. I watched Big Dick pull his arm away from one man's grip. I didn't bother with goodbyes. He didn't either. He just gave me one last look and shook his head. One last final disappointment. For once however, probably the first

time in my life, I genuinely didn't give a shit.

I took a seat on the couch. I was overcome with tiredness, but I hadn't even settled on the real matter at hand. Veronica took a seat in the chair where Big Dick had sat. She looked engulfed by the large armchair, all but her frizzy ball of hair at the top of her head. I couldn't hear voices or movement in the other room. I stayed silent and listened out for the men to return. Veronica sat looking at me. I grew uncomfortable in the silence. I always did. I'm one of those guys that needs background noise at all times and I never know what to do with my hands. I folded them first on my lap. Then laid them flat on my knees. Then I swung them across my chest, but realized how defensive that made me look, so I dropped them to my sides again. Surely you get the point. Veronica sensed my anxiety, I know it. Finally she said, 'They're not coming back.'

'Who's not?'

She scrunched her eyebrows. 'My friends. Who do you think? Not now at least.'

'Will they really let Big Dick go?'

'They will. They're not going to let him walk away out of here though. They'll drop him somewhere inconvenient.'

'What the hell does that accomplish?'

'Well, for starters, it buys all of us some time before he's picked up by the cops. He will try to roll us all. I'm serious about that.'

'Yeah, I know that.' I said.

'That includes you too Ricky.'

'Believe me. I'm well aware of what he's capable of. There are no more misconceptions concerning my old man.'

'Maybe, maybe not.'

I'd had enough of talking about my Dad. I guess I'd always known that someday there'd be repercussions for being Big Dick's kid. I just never could figure how they would materialize. I'd gone on long enough in the dark. I was tired and I needed answers. 'Do you want to stop bullshitting me now Veronica?'

'Bullshitting you? Nothing I've ever said or done to you has been bullshit.'

'Well, there's never been the whole truth either though has there? Admit that at least. Come on. Rich girl playing poor barmaid. Not to mention a girl who seems to know everyone everywhere. Stop bullshitting me, like I said. Who the hell are you?'

'I'm exactly who I appear to be Ricky. Who the

fuck are you? That's the question. I'm only ever one Veronica. I don't change my personality to suit anyone anywhere. You're the one hiding behind a facade most of your life.'

'What the fuck are you talking about? Honestly, I want to know what's going on. Who's reading what I'm writing? Who's . . . you know, acting on it? It's your fucking network or whatever you call it. Your people. Probably your fixers. That's it isn't it. You've got fixers, just like Big Dick, only broader, more geographically diverse. By extension, I'm guessing more sophisticated and dangerous. Jesus Christ Veronica, I read in the *Blackpool Times* that Bud Kershaw got gutted by a smuggled blade in a Texas prison. Bud fucking Kershaw. No one in Blackpool ever even heard of this guy until I stumbled across some blog post on him. Now he's worthy of local news. And he's fucking dead. I'm not Big Dick. I don't want some guy's blood on my hands, whether he's an asshole or not.'

'Ricky, I'm sure Bud Kershaw had plenty more enemies close to home. He didn't need some obscure article written thousands of miles away to draw attention to himself.'

'So you're saying you know nothing about this

then?'

'That's not what I'm saying. I know everything about this. I'm saying Bud Kershaw was probably a coincidence though.'

'Probably?'

She shrugged, 'Who can know for sure?'

I rubbed my eyes hard with the palms of my hands. I was running in circles and my head was hurting worse by the second. 'Veronica, please, just tell me what's going on here.'

'Well, I hope it's the start of a revolution.'

'A revolution? Who's revolting? You saying you have what . . . like an army?'

'It's more like a web.'

'So you know people everywhere? Across the country? You put this web together?'

'Me? No. It's not something that was put together, not by me at least. And I don't personally know that many people outside this city's limits. This kind of web just forms.'

'So who is it? They? Them, I mean.'

'It's not really them or they. Think of it as being you or me.'

'You're being cryptic.'

'You're being unimaginative and obtuse.'

'Am I?'

'You are indeed, yes.'

'Fine, let's say I'm obtuse. Let's try something more specific though. Who are these fixers and what do they do?'

She let out a sigh. She looked like a child resigned to telling the truth to her parents. 'What they do is varied and tough to pin down. Who they are is easy. Like I said, they're you and me or people just like us. They were sold a lie all their lives about what success was and what happiness looked like. So they near killed themselves getting there only to feel utterly empty. You could say, they're the beguiled above average, the easily swayed, the groomed for white-collar, middle management, cookie-cutter administration connoisseurs. They're the ones that listened to guidance counsellors, teachers, aunts, uncles, mentors, whoever, instead of listening to themselves, their own hearts. They're like you Ricky, artists, writers, painters, craftsmen, bakers, chefs, you name it, that are dressed up instead in ill-fitting suits and ties, uncomfortable, unhealthy, unhappy, sleep walking through day after tedious day, hiding their true selves, suppressing their true personality, all to fit some inoffensive and vanilla white corporate fucking mold. Meanwhile their companies and their government are busy raping the public, forcing them into debt, and doing their very best to keep the entire population enslaved by an idea of happiness instead of the real fucking thing. And just like you Ricky, these people are angry. Every one of these fixers if you want to call them that, are really fucking angry. And spiteful. And what's happening is that a reckoning is coming because they know things. They know a lot of interesting things. These people know where the cracks are in the system, the combinations to the safe, the blank checks, the invoices that just get paid because computer says pay. Despite their boredom and self-loathing, they're sponges, soaking up inside information. Every company has them, they're hidden in plain sight. They're intelligent, competent and angry soaked sponges of information.'

I sat up straight to listen to Veronica's speech. It was a departure from her typical brevity. I sat for a full two minutes afterwards, absorbing what she had said. I needed a drink badly, but my legs were like jelly and I didn't want to get up and wobble to the kitchen for one. 'So, what am I then? Some kind of messenger?'

She shook her head. 'The message is already out there. It's already spread. You're not a messenger

Ricky. You're a medium.'

'What is it you want me to do then? What the hell can I really do with this?'

'That's easy.' She said. 'You're doing it already. Just keep squeezing the fucking sponge.'

'So you want me to keep writing? With all this shit going on, you want me to just keep doing what I'm doing, hiding out, laying low and writing whatever comes to mind?'

'While you can, yes. Except I want you to do it faster and be more specific.'

I put my hands on my knees and leaned forward. 'I saw beer bottles in the kitchen. Is there more?'

She shrugged. 'Check the fridge. There was some in there. We had to keep Big Dick on the level.'

I stood up and walked into the kitchen. I needed a minute to think more than anything. Fixers, webs, networks, whatever they are or are not, they sounded weird and foreign to me. At the same time I couldn't disagree with what she was saying. Are there worse things in life than being bored and misled, yes of course, much worse. Does that make it right? In my mind no, somebody or something, somewhere for chrissakes, should hang for the system that he or they created and sustain. I opened the fridge and pulled out two beers. I twisted the top off of one and took a long gulp. I pulled the bottle from my mouth when I heard a noise behind me. I turned and Veronica stood an arm's length away looking at me.

'You want one?' I asked and held out the unopened bottle towards her.

She shook her head. 'I don't drink.' She said.

'Really? What, you're an alcoholic or something like that?'

'No, I quit drinking so I could look down my nose at those that do.'

'Oh.' I said. 'Good. That working out for you?'

'Makes me feel good.' She said.

'That's important.'

'Listen Ricky, I know what you're thinking. You're considering whether or not this is something you want to be a part of, but you're forgetting one big thing. You're already a part of this. A big part. These are your people.'

'Come on. These aren't my people. Your people maybe.'

'No, they're your people in that you're one of them Ricky. These are people just like you. You're in this already.'

'I'm in this thanks to you and Big Dick.'

'Ricky, no one's ever had a gun to your head telling you what to do. Not ever. You're into what you're into on your own accord. Thinking anything to the contrary is just you fooling yourself.'

'All right, fine. For argument's sake, let's say I'm one of these "fixers". What's so new or unique about them? There's always some revolt somewhere, some generation bucking the trend of the last, raging against the machine. What's different about now?'

'The now is different, that's it. You're right, there's always some group out there pushing back on the establishment. That's not new. They've always been around, it's the times that change. People say to strike when the time is right. I don't think that's effective. Or at least it's very hard to judge. I would advocate you keep striking, continuously, over and over again and hope that time catches up. Plus, Ricky, we're not talking about hacktivists here. Well, not exclusively. This group is different. They're a hybrid. Sure, there are plenty out there that can steal your password, empty your bank account and post pictures of cocks to your Facebook page. But, for every one of those, there are five others that would just as easily set fire to your building.'

'They sound like terrorists.'

'They're activists or call them revolutionaries. There is a line, but I'll agree at times it grows very thin.'

'I don't know Veronica. I may feel strongly about some things, but I'm not out looking to hurt anyone, you know?'

'No one ever is. You're here because you want to be here. The moment you don't want that, you should leave. But do so knowing this is as much your fight as anyone else's.'

'Except I don't know who or what we're fighting.'

'Maybe not specifically, but you do understand why you're fighting. To me that's more important.'

I leaned up against the sink and finished my beer. I tipped the bottle upside down in the basin with the other empties. I pointed to the accumulation of beer bottles. 'How long was he here anyhow?'

'Not long enough to justify the volume of booze he took in.'

I nodded my head in agreement. Honestly, I was coming around to the idea of being a part of something. For once in my life I felt a kinship with others, even if I didn't know any of them personally, the idea of being part of a group was comforting. I'd always felt alone. That feeling only grew in magnitude as the years ticked by. Veronica held up her hand as if to say stay put. She walked into her bedroom and came out a few seconds later with a man's hat and a light jacket in her hands. She handed them to me.

'Put these on.' She said. 'I want to show you something.'

'What?' I said. 'Where?'

'Close by. Don't worry, we'll drive.'

'But, is it safe?'

'Hence the disguise. Put it on.' She said. I trusted her innately at this stage. I couldn't tell you why, but I think it's mainly just that I wanted to be able to trust her, so I did. I took off my trendy sports jacket and put the other one on. The collar was higher on the new one and it had a hood, which I kept off, but liked knowing it was there. I put the hat on and kept it low so it cut off the ends of my eyebrows from view. I followed her once again through her bedroom and out the window. I was used to the fire escape by now. Its sense of adventure had worn off. The climb down was mechanical. I imagined it's how firemen felt about sliding down the pole after a few years on the job. We walked quickly down the alleyway to the small side street where her car was parked. There was

no sign of the cops watching the building. I wondered for a few seconds whether it was all just a ruse. I wondered if the cops were really looking for me or not. It could be bullshit. I wouldn't be able to tell the difference, I never gave them the chance to ask any questions. Then it dawned on me that I didn't mind if that part of it all was made up. I'd be a fool to want the cops to be out searching for me, especially for something I had nothing to do with. Compared to my normal life, my current circumstance was an adventure. Sure, I was worried, mostly the worry was about potentially being locked up. I realized suddenly that despite the stress and worry I was actually enjoying this. My newest fear was that this adventure would eventually have to come to an end. I pushed the thought aside for the moment. It would end surely, but not yet. I wasn't ready for it to end quite yet.

Veronica weaved quickly through the back streets of the city. We spilled out onto a highway heading west. She pulled off after only one or two exits. Although we were within earshot to the city, the surroundings off of the exit were green and rolling. There were low green mountains in the distance that gave the area a country feel. She turned onto a road

guarded by stone gates, though they were opened and we drove straight through. It was an industrial estate of some kind, though it was sprawling with tree-lined roads and manmade lakes and fountains. The buildings within it were sparse. The entire area gave off the impression of being a model, some kind of fictional estate, designed for a sales pitch. We drove for a few more minutes until Veronica pulled the car to a stop on the side of the road across from a large, low-rise building. It looked like an airplane hangar designed by a trendy architect. She put the car in park and pulled the keys from the ignition.

'Well?' I said. I had expected some revelation upon getting where we were going. Staring at the mundane building in a pristine business park didn't give me that "Ah ha" moment I had anticipated. She opened the door and climbed out.

'Let's sit.' She said. I got out of the car after her and followed her over to a bench that looked across at the same building.

'I can't say I really get whatever message you're trying to send.' I said.

'Do you see that building?' She asked.

'The one right in front of us?' I pointed. 'Yes.'

'What's odd about it to you?' I looked the

building up and down and side to side. I did get a sense of something being wrong, but I couldn't place it. I never was very good at *Where's Waldo.* I closed my eyes for a second, then something occurred to me.

'The cars.' I said.

'What about them?'

I counted the cars in the parking lot. 'There are only three that I can see. It's a weekday during office hours. It's a large building, I'd expect more people in it.'

'Good.' She said. 'Anything else?'

I looked again. I noticed the stone pillar next to the security barrier. There was a number on it, carved into the stone, but nothing else. 'There's no sign of a company name or logo. Also, there's no obvious building name. It's like the building doesn't want to be found.'

'Very good.' Veronica said.

'Do I get a prize?'

She took out a usb memory key and handed it to me. 'Here's your prize. Keep it safe.

I looked it over then put it in my pocket. 'What's on it?' I asked.

'A few things, company names, addresses, directions, building blueprints, things like that for

hundreds of these buildings across the globe.

'And that's important?'

'That stick could get you killed.' She said. 'Keep it close.'

'So then, what is this plan?'

'You heard of cloud computing?'

I shrugged. I'd heard the name, but the topic never warranted my attention. 'Okay, sure, not enough to converse on it.'

'Don't worry, all you need to know is that this building is the "cloud". It's a sterile, secure building with wall to wall computer servers.'

'Okay, fine. I still don't know why I should give a shit.'

Veronica shook her head in disappointment. 'It's the data Ricky. Everything is stored here or in buildings just like it around the world. There's an area west of Dublin in Ireland were all your major software companies have these buildings. It doesn't get too hot or too cold there, so they save millions on air conditioning. Meanwhile the concentration of data centers is slowly destroying the landscape and the climate, but it's all good because the Irish government and the EPA are paid to look the other way. They're also paid to prioritize electricity and

other emergency services so that they get sent straight to the data centers in the event of a disaster. Never mind the hospitals, the people in distress, it's the data that needs saving. Keep the data up and running so the software companies can keep making money from other corporations and governments, that's the priority. Fuck the people. That very same scenario is playing out in several cities and countries across the globe.

'So it's company data being held in here?'

'Yes, but it's much more than that. I guarantee you, you're information is in there. Your name, email address, all your passwords, your contacts, known associates, religion, political beliefs, sexual orientation, whether or not you have a pet or drink alcohol or buy brand name jeans, you name it. Yes, they have that on you and millions upon millions of other people. The basic stuff you assume, sure no harm, but this goes way beyond basic. As long as you're a subject in a file within that building, you're a slave. You don't control any aspect of your life. What you buy, where you go on vacation, what you think, how feel from one moment to the next. It's all manufactured through here, synthesized emotions. You're a commodity being bought and sold to the

highest bidder or bidders, over and over again.'

'Jesus.' I said.

'Yes, Jesus. And that's before we get into the realm of which governments across the globe have easy access to this. They're probably the highest bidders. That is unless they just take the information without paying for it, which is typically how they'll go about it. If they can't gather their own data on you, which they usually can, they'll just buy it or take it from the information supermarket.'

It was a lot to take in, but I didn't need much convincing. It's fair to say I've always had a rubber arm when it comes to blaming the establishment. Where there's smoke, there's fire. These innocuous buildings had within them unchecked power over millions, maybe billions of individuals. There was no more off the grid. The grid spans every corner of the earth. I reached into my pocket and pulled out the memory key.

'So you want me to write a piece on data centers? Their . . . evils, and post it with all this? The names and locations of buildings like these all over the world?' I asked.

'Exactly.'

I thought more about it. This was well beyond

what I'd done so far. This was not local, random and unsolved. This was global and specific. If my impact as a medium stayed consistent, it was incendiary.

'If things operate as before, this could have consequences.' I said.

'I'm counting on it.'

'There's a word for this Veronica.'

'Yes. It's called a revolution.'

'I had a different word in mind.'

'Come Ricky. A terrorist doesn't give a fuck about change. A terrorist just wants to act out some violent fantasy. That's why you see Isis shooting at innocent civilians in Paris or tourists in North Africa. They're out for blood and violence, not real action. Otherwise, they'd be out to get the establishment, not the people.'

'The line is blurry Veronica.'

'But, there is a line, I assure you. Heroes and criminals aren't truly defined until the outcome is decided.'

I scratched my head. 'History is written by the winners, in other words.'

'For better or worse, yes.'

'What if there are no winners?'

'Then the fight's not over Ricky. So it's not

history yet.'

11

It was less than an hour before I was back in Veronica's mansion in front of a laptop screen. I was seated again at the large mahogany desk, working through the wording of the opening paragraph in my head. I looked out the large window. I could see the black Mercedes in its usual spot. I could even make out the two shapes in the front seat. It all seemed normal and familiar at this stage. I felt like the last few hours could have occurred in a day dream, except that I couldn't get the stink of Big Dick's cinnamon whiskey out of my nose. I took my time with this article. The pacing needed to work. I needed enough detail to provide context, but not so much that someone less technically inclined might just gloss over with boredom. There needed to be sufficient build up that accelerated to a climax. Veronica sat in a chair watching me work. She read over my shoulder occasionally and gave me comments as I wrote. I found that part of the process irritating except that each time she leaned in I could smell her perfume and lip gloss. That aspect I enjoyed thoroughly. She backed off after most of the text was formulated, but chimed in again when it came to the placement of the memory key's contents. She wanted the reader to have no choice but to look at the data center locations. It had to immediately follow the description of evils, the punchline. The reader needed to think this is terrible, then immediately see if this was happening in his or her own backyard. In that way Veronica seemed to stay true to at least one element of news reporting, if it was local, people will take it seriously.

An hour or two after it started, there was a completed draft. I slid the chair back and stretched out my arms then my fingers. Veronica stayed seated watching me.

'Finished?' She asked.

'First draft.' I said, then I stood up.

'Where are you going?'

'What?' I need to walk away for a little while, come back with a fresh set of eyes for a cold read before putting it out there. It's my routine.'

She shook her head. 'Ricky. You haven't been doing this long enough to pick up a routine. Let me read it. I've got fresh eyes.'

'You've been staring at the screen as long as I have, what are you talking about? What's the rush? It's written, it'll be out soon enough.'

'What's the rush?' She said. Her face was turning red. The word incredulous came to mind. 'Ricky, any second Big Dick could get picked up and we're shut down. This needs to be out before that. That's my rush.'

She reached over for the mouse and I panicked. I reached out and grabbed her wrist. She looked up at me. Her face registered surprise at first, then anger. I never saw her other hand move. She reached out and grabbed my package. I let out a yelp that descended into a whimper as she squeezed harder. I slowly let go of her wrist. She stayed holding on tight. I couldn't speak. I watched her move the mouse. She scrolled down and hovered over the world "Publish". She clicked the mouse. I watched the swirling ball on screen as it loaded. A few seconds later, the message came on screen, "Congratulations, your post was published." I felt the grip on my nuts ease from a squeeze and twist to a firm cupping. The associated

pain subsided. Her hand lingered on my crotch. Blood began flowing to all extremities as I was still looking at the laptop. I turned my head away from the screen and towards Veronica's face. Her eyes seemed to pierce through my own. Still her hand hadn't moved away. My arousal was no longer a secret, to put it lightly. Her face lightened into a smile. She finally removed her hand, but it didn't go far. She grabbed my belt loop and pulled me towards her. She met me half way with her lips. I wish I could tell you that we both succumbed to euphoric love making, but I haven't lied to you yet, so I won't start now. We had sex, just to clear the air, it did happen. Veronica led me into the bedroom, her mouth firmly attached to mine most of the way. Her frizzy hair loosened and fell to her shoulders when I pulled her shirt over her head. It's painful to remember how beautiful she looked at that moment. Really my only regret is how quickly the entire thing came to a close. I think I even gave her the "it's not, you it's me" line, which in retrospect was painfully accurate and obvious to all parties involved. Afterwards she was sweet. She even continued to kiss me a little bit and let my hand linger on her bare thigh.

It was the perfect culmination of a long and

eventful day, one full of revelation after revelation. The emotional roller coaster of an afternoon took its toll on me. Laying there next to Veronica, engulfed in the scent of her perfume and warmed by the skin on skin contact really soothed my soul. Nothing else mattered to me at the time. Only the moment alone was important. I drifted off asleep eventually. It was barely dark out when I did, but the curtains were pulled in the bedroom and the masked sunset did enough to send me snoring away in the arms of my sociopathic angel.

I woke up with a start sometime later. Something caused me to wake abruptly, but at the time I wasn't sure what. I was disoriented. It was dark at last and I was sweating. It could've been ten pm or two am. I couldn't even wager a guess. Between nightfall and sun up the city always sounded more or less the same. I had an odd feeling that something was wrong, but couldn't tell what. It's that deep reptilian brain telling you that the oven's still on or the iron was left plugged in. I felt nauseous all of a sudden and thought I'd get sick. It passed after a few seconds and I realized it was hunger. I found my clothes on the floor and put them on. There was no sign of Veronica or her clothes in the bedroom. I pictured her waking up in a storm

of regret, sick at the thought of me and running out of the house. It left a lingering dread hanging over me. I headed downstairs. I was startled by the echo of my own footsteps. The mansion felt more empty than it had just hours before. It had seemed almost like home while I worked on the article with Veronica at my side. Remembering the piece I wrote and Veronica's insistence to publish immediately tickled a niggling doubt in the back of my mind. Downstairs the floor was cold on my bare feet and it made me shiver. I crept into the dark kitchen. The small light above the oven shone dimly in the room. Everything outside of the light's two foot diameter was covered in darkness. I slid my hand along the wall reaching for the light switch. I found it and flicked it on. The glare from the steel appliances left stars in my eyes. The kitchen looked freshly cleaned, which was not how I'd left it. That was odd. I opened the refrigerator. It was empty. All the remaining food had been cleared out. I was confused. I felt beads of sweat develop on my forehead. I walked around the rest of the first floor turning lights on. I hadn't ventured often outside the kitchen, so I couldn't judge whether anything was different. I abandoned the downstairs and ran up the staircase. I turned the bathroom light on. It was as

bare and clean as the kitchen. It had been emptied out. I opened the wardrobe. All the clothes were gone. I caught sight of my reflection in the mirror and realized for the first time that I was wearing the clothes that I had on when Veronica's goons first picked me up and took me to the mansion. I didn't know what this meant. I started pinching myself. It wasn't a dream, that much I was sure of. I went back into the bedroom and found my shoes and jacket. I got fully dressed, disappointed that my stylish wardrobe was gone. In my old clothes, I felt like the poor sap I'd always been. I needed to get out of there. Something was wrong. I'd been screwed over enough in my life to know whatever was happening now was not working out for my benefit.

I ran out into the hallway and headed for the stairs. I paused at the doorway to the office. It looked the same as it always had. I stared into the room, surprised to see the laptop still sitting opened on the large mahogany desk. I walked into the room and hovered over the machine. Then I thought of something. I cupped my hands and put them against the window. I looked out to the street. The Mercedes was gone. It wasn't until then that I felt well and truly alone. I walked over to the laptop and moved the

mouse to bring the screen up. When it started up, I saw the page that Veronica and I had published earlier was still opened. I scrolled down. There were more comments than I could count. I kept clicking the "read more" button and more would appear. They were endless. I navigated to the stats page. I was surprised by the noise my sharp intake of breath produced. The page views had spiked well beyond everything we had done previously combined. It was in the millions and climbing. I took a seat and watched the view counter tick away. I thought back to the article's content, the global nature of the concern we highlighted. The magnitude of what we had done began to hit me.

Suddenly, the page went blank. I scratched my head for a second. I checked the wireless signal. It seemed to be working. I typed in the web address again and hit "enter". An error message came on screen. I tried a few more sites, mostly news or social media websites. Each one I went to appeared to have the same error screen. I checked the wireless again. It was still a strong signal. I restarted the laptop and checked again. It was the same. I was assuming it was some issue with the network or with the computer itself, that is until I heard the rumble of an

explosion in the distance. My heart was racing. I looked out the window but couldn't see far past the trees out the back. I ran downstairs and pushed opened the front door. I ran down to the lawn. On lower ground I didn't have a quality view in every direction, but the night sky was clear except for a cloud of grey smoke rising to the moon from the west of the city. At that moment, my fears were realized. The seeds of doubt and regret were heaved to the forefront of my mind. I knew what had happened. I assumed it was now happening all over the world. Explosions would be going off in unsettled suburbs where cheap unwanted land was given over to corporate America for building their information palaces. I was hoping these places were remotely monitored so that no one was inside at the point of explosion, otherwise there was no way to wipe the blood from my hands on this one. I left the mansion and set off in a sprint back across the river. A man, fully dressed sprinting down the street in the middle of the night was attention seeking, but I didn't care. I reached the river and ran across the foot bridge. My steps pounded off the floating steel. The force of my steps reverberated through my knees. I didn't bother with back alleyways and subtleties. I ran straight for

the Harlot's Den. I saw the neon sign for it ahead and ran harder. I reached Veronica's apartment entrance and pushed through the door quickly. Inside, the lone lightbulb must have flickered to its death. I couldn't see anything. I kicked my way over to the staircase. I could feel my heartbeat pulsing in my ears as I climbed the steps. It blocked out any other noise. At the top of the stairs I knocked loudly. I waited just a few seconds, then pounded on the door again. I stepped back for leverage to kick the door in. Then I paused. I reached out and turned the knob. It twisted and the door opened with a creak.

I stepped into the hallway. Inside was cold and my footsteps echoed. I approached like a detective on a cop show, hugging tightly to the wall before swinging around the corner of a doorway. I did so without a gun of course. I checked the kitchen first, then the living room. Both rooms were empty of people and belongings. The apartment had been cleared out. I had a sinking feeling in my stomach. I walked into what was previously Veronica's bedroom. I thought I could still faintly smell her perfume, but it was probably my imagination. I walked back out to the hallway. I slumped against the wall and sat on the floor. I felt about as empty as the apartment. I was

confused. I felt anger and sadness. Tears formed in my eyes. I looked up at the wall above the kitchen doorway. The strange cross with Chinese-looking writing was still hanging there. I wiped my tears and stood up. I walked over to look more closely at the forgotten artifact. I looked at the Chinese characters. I stared at them like one would at a magic eye poster until I realized they were no more Chinese than the fortune cookie. I reached up and tilted the cross to the side. When I did so, the message written in an odd script was clear and it was very much in English. It read "Go fuck yourself".

I couldn't help but smile through my pain. I took my hand away and let the cross slide back to its resting position, masking its profane greeting. I stood for a minute in silence waiting for an idea of what to do next. I was blank. My nerves were shot and I was defeated. I floated towards the front door back into the darkness of the entrance hall and staircase. I kept my palms tight to each side of the wall as I descended. Close to the bottom I notice the dangling bulb began to flicker once again. The light it produced was dim. It appeared to be fighting for its life. I stood watching it for a minute. It reminded me of what a bee looks like on the ground after you've

swatted it, but it didn't die. I always feel sorry for the bee when that happens. I regret immediately swatting it down, so much so that I agonize over giving it the final death blow. The flickering light bulb brought me the same agony. The helpless creature emitting its last glow before entering the darkness for good. I felt I had to stay with it until the end. The end came only a few seconds later. It left me in darkness once again except for a dull reflection of the Harlot's Den neon sign bouncing off of the slick ground out front.

I opened the door and stepped out. I breathed in the now familiar stank of urine and stale booze. I stood under the neon lights not knowing where to go or what to do. I was angry at her disappearing, but I missed Veronica already. I even thought having Big Dick around at that moment would give me comfort. I heard a car door slam close by and suddenly snapped to attention. I hadn't noticed when I stepped outside a dark sedan parked diagonally across the street. Two men were walking towards me. Neither looked familiar, but I saw the gleam of metal on the waist of one. I couldn't tell if it was a badge or a gun, but I guessed he had both. I froze with panic. Another sedan pulled around the corner at the same time. I took a few steps backwards into the shadow of

Veronica's doorway. The door to the second car opened and I made eye contact with O'Brien. 'Oh fucking bollocks' I thought. O'Brien jumped out of the car and called my name. I saw the two men walking towards me start moving faster. 'Fuck this.' I said out loud. I turned and ran back into the hallway and up the stairs. I heard O'Brien shouting orders to the men to follow me in. I kept on running and pushed through the door, then slammed it shut behind me. I could already hear the men running up the stairs behind me. There was a deadbolt attached to the door, which I slid into place. It would buy me thirty seconds to a minute. I ran through the hallway and kitchen and straight into Veronica's old bedroom. I struggled to pry the old window open, but got it after a few seconds. I climbed out onto the fire escape and forced the window down again. I began climbing down. I couldn't hear the men behind me yet, but I knew they'd be coming soon. All I could hear was own breath and the clanging of metal from my weight bouncing down the fire escape. I got to the last ladder and jumped down. I landed hard and felt my ankle twist. I got up and hobbled towards the end of the alleyway. I made it to the dumpster before I heard O'Brien yell for me to stop. He had a gun pointed at

me and was less than ten feet away. I slowly resigned myself to my fate. I could hear the others working open the creaky window from Veronica's room. I stayed frozen next to the dumpster and what looked to be a pile of trash and old blankets. My eyes stayed fixed on O'Brien's gun. He took a step towards me. I heard a loud bang and my heart nearly stopped. I thought my ear drum was blown and I could hear ringing in both ears. O'Brien's gun dropped to his side and he fell to the ground holding his shin. I could see blood leaking out through his fingers just below his knee. The pile of trash and blankets next to me began to move and change shape. I stayed frozen. My feet were glued from fear to the concrete under my shoes. As the figure emerged from the trash pile I caught a scent of cinnamon whiskey. My eyes widened in surprise. Big Dick stood up. The shitty blankets fell from his shoulders to expose his large frame that loomed over O'Brien on the ground writhing in pain. A .38 revolver stayed pointed at O'Brien. He took another step towards him. I could see O'Brien raise a hand in front of his face. It was a feeble attempt to ward off a closing shot.

'I've had enough of this fucking bollocks.' Big Dick said. It was more to himself than anybody else.

He took another step forward and stuck the gun about a foot from O'Brien's head. Time seemed to stand still. I knew right then that Big Dick wasn't done. There was no ambiguity in his posture.

'Dad!' I yelled. Big Dick didn't move. I saw his arm stiffen and thought I saw his thumb move to cock the revolver, but I can't be sure. I darted towards him and dove. My footsteps must have registered because he turned in my direction. I wrapped my arms around him when I struck him. He was much bigger than me, but his balance was not reliable. For once I thanked his cinnamon whiskey habit. He fell over and I fell on top of him. I heard the gun rattle off of the concrete and I braced myself expecting a shot to let loose. None did thankfully. Big Dick fought me for a second. I threw a punch or two, but then just held on for dear life. I hugged him as tightly as I could for as long as I could. I could feel my last bit of energy draining as he continued to fight me. Seconds later multiple sets of arms grabbed me and pulled me to my feet. I knew my arms were restrained and felt pressure around my wrists, which in retrospect were handcuffs. Whether from the fear or just the exhaustion, a few seconds later I went limp and blacked out.

12

Seagulls, sirens and trains, that's all I heard for nearly two weeks. And voices too I suppose, but they're always mumbled or sandwiched on top of other voices so that I couldn't make out a single line of dialogue. How can one not remain in a melancholic state given those circumstances? When I hear seagulls calling in the distance I'm transported back to youthful summer days spent on the beach. I can almost taste the salty warm breeze, feel the sand underneath my toes, and hear my mother's voice again, God rest her soul, calling for me so I don't wander too far away as the ocean's tide slowly drifts me in one or another direction. A siren will sound in the distance and dissolve that memory into another, one of lying awake at night listening to the ambulances pull in and out of the Catholic teaching hospital that was less than a mile away from our apartment. The rumble of the train tracks followed on from the same memory to my teenage years growing up adjacent to the train station that led into Blackpool's city center. Normally that onset of nostalgia would leave me smiling and peaceful, however juxtaposed against three stone walls and a sealed heavy door they left me incredibly somber. Unless you're where you want to be, with who you want to be with, I find that good memories often bring more pain than relief.

As I suspected, data centers worldwide were attacked by my Fixers. Yes, I see them as mine now. No one knew for certain how many or how severe those attacks were or how they actually materialized. The flow of information globally was slowed to a crawl. My guess is there was a cyber mission first to cause confusion and concern before the actual bombs started going off. I thought of it as the jab jab, before the right cross. From what I understood there was pandemonium on the streets, but that was hearsay, basically information I gleaned from the types of questions I was asked during interrogation sessions. I could hear the streets and to me they sounded pretty normal. Not once in two weeks have I heard anyone

howling at the moon and I was in Blackpool Police Plaza on the worst street in the city. I got the sense they couldn't move me to an actual prison because with the systems down, they weren't sure how to process the paperwork. It was a bureaucratic cluster fuck. I imagined Veronica was somewhere laughing her ass off.

I expected a visit from the FBI, but to date I'd only seen and heard from a handful of Blackpool detectives. Most of the questions they asked still related to the shooting on the riverfront. I could see their irritation building at my genuine lack of information. I asked them about Big Dick, but they gave me nothing. I guessed he was somewhere in the building, but I couldn't hear him or smell him. I was still trying to convince myself I didn't care. I longed to see Veronica, to talk to her again, understand her motives, even just breathe in the aroma from her perfume and lip gloss that haunted my dreams. If I couldn't see her again, I at least wanted those dreams to continue.

I heard the shake of keys outside my door and then a heavy latch turned over. I sat up on the hard bed and planted my feet on the floor. The sound of someone opening the door caught me by surprise.

The timing of it was outside of the routine that had developed. I tensed like a cornered squirrel and waited for the door to open. I saw a young policeman in the doorway. I could see another one just to the left of it. Both men slowly entered the room.

'Stand up Sherman.' He said.

'What's this?' I asked.

'Relax.' He said. 'Turn around and hands on the top of your head. Don't lock your fingers.'

I complied, but I wasn't happy about it. The officer reached out and grabbed my arm. He pulled it back and I felt the cuff wrap around my wrist. I heard the click of the metal, then he did the same with the other arm.

'Am I being moved?' I asked as he walked me out of the room and into the hall. Out in the hall I could voices from outside the building. It sounded like chanting, more like a protest than a riot. I couldn't make out the chant's slogan.

'You're staying with us for now. It's your lawyer that's all. He said you'd be expecting him. He apologized for the delay.'

'My lawyer?' I asked. The officer gave me a look. I could see he was considering the question. I gave him a tight smile. 'It's about time.' I said.

They walked me down the hallway and through the main lobby. I could see briefly through the front door there was some kind of crowd gathered, but I still couldn't make out what they were chanting. There was a semi-circle of cops guarding the entrance from the inside of the building. On the other side of the lobby, there was another hall with a set of interview rooms. I knew the area from my several interviews with the detectives. The cops led me over to one of the interview rooms. Before entering I turned and asked the young cop, 'Any word on O'Brien?'

He looked at me funny. He must have thought I was being sarcastic. He just shrugged and said. 'Crutches.'

I nodded and decided not to probe for more information. My concern was genuine, but he'd never be convinced of that. They walked me into the room and sat me down on a chair in front of steel table. One of the cops hooked my cuffs to a latch on the table. My lawyer stood with his back to me looking at a camera in the corner of the room. The young cop cleared his throat to get the man's attention. The man turned around. He didn't look at me. I stared at him and tried not to look surprised.

'I hope that doesn't also record sound?' He asked one of the cops.

'Not as a default.' The cop said. 'Video only.'

'Be sure of it.' The man said. 'Otherwise the city of Blackpool will be naming this building after me and you'll be picking up dog shit along the river the rest of your career.'

The cop didn't respond. He stood staring at the lawyer.

'Leave us.' The lawyer said. He slid into the chair across from me at the table.

'There's a buzzer under the table.' The cop said. 'Under your knee. We're right outside.'

The two cops left the room then and closed the door. The man waited a few seconds after the door was closed before speaking.

'How are you holding up?' He asked.

'Green Peter.' I said. 'You're a lawyer?'

'I'm a lot of things, whatever the circumstances call for.'

'Did Veronica . . .' I started to ask.

He shook his head. 'Sorry Sherman. No one's seen or heard from her.'

I took in a deep breath. 'Then who sent you?'

'Who? I sent me. Don't you know Sherman?

You're the voice son. The prophet. This revolution's only just begun.'

I sat and stared at him for any signs of sarcasm or irony. I found none. I could feel my hands starting to shake. It was adrenaline, nervous excitement, a realization that I wasn't as alone as I thought. I felt a lump in my throat. I felt the onset of tears and choked them back before Green Peter saw them and changed his mind. In our silence I heard the chanting from outside the building grow louder and louder. The voices seemed to be closing in, growing more violent.

'So what happens now?' I asked.

'Wait for it.' He said.

I wanted to ask 'wait for what' but I didn't. I didn't need to. A moment later the room went dark. I couldn't see anything at first, then I saw a flash of a pen light in Green Peter's fist. It shone on my own hands as he undid the lock on my cuffs. I heard a commotion outside the room echoing through the halls. There were yells and screams. It sounded like a crowd at the Colosseum. It seemed to get louder and louder, then pass outside the hall carrying away the noise with it. My wrists were free. Green Peter pulled me to my feet and led me by the arm to the door. He opened it and led me into the hall. It looked like a mob passed through it. There was no sign of the young officers that were guarding the door or anyone else for that matter. I could still hear the chanting nearby.

'Follow me.' Peter said. He moved quickly and repeatedly looked back to be sure I kept up. We weaved through the depths of the police station, through ransacked offices and turned over vending machines. I could hear yelling and cries for help. I ignored them and continued following Green Peter. Finally we reached the end of the building. He led me out a back door. We ran between several parked cruisers and slipped out onto the street through an opening that had been cut out from the steel gate. Out on the street a car sped up to us and then slammed on its brakes. A door flung open and Green Peter jumped in. I followed right behind him. I sat back in the seat and the car sped off.

The man in the passenger seat turned around and smiled. 'We got you Sherman.' He said.

I nodded in thanks. I turned around and looked out the back window. I could see the crowd was still assembled and chanting. I never did find out what they were saying.

'Are those your people?' I asked Green Peter.

He laughed. 'They might've started that way. They're your people now too.'

It dawned on me finally that not only was I not alone, I was also free. I smiled. 'I never imagined I'd have a following.'

'What do you mean Sherman, didn't see the black community getting behind you?'

'I meant any following. Anybody.' I said.

'You think you can be the voice for the minority groups too?' The man driving the car asked.

I shrugged. I looked over at Green Peter. 'Let me ask you a question. Do you think that when we finally make contact with aliens from beyond this planet, all this bullshit about race and religious differences becomes superfluous?'

Green Peter laughed. 'Maybe Sherman. I doubt it, but maybe. Either that or it's just another group to hate.'

<u>THE END</u>

BLACKPOOL KNIGHTS (A SAMPLE)

CHAPTER 1

GRAFTON HALIFAX

The man crouched next to a stone staircase. A ledge over his head gave him shelter, but the worn stone still leaked in several spots and rusty water dripped onto the blanket that covered his shoulders. He wore a black wool hat with long hair sprouting from the back and a dark beard covered the lower half of his face. He'd been watching the building across the street for weeks, but still hadn't seen the man he came to kill. It was a man with no real name, referred to only as The Pelican. He never showed his face in public. Everyone knew he existed, but no one knew him to see him, not the cops, not even his own mother.

Girls entered the building in packs and they stayed for long shifts. Men came alone and stayed for no more than an hour, usually less and always with a look of hesitation walking in and one of nonchalance coming out. Those movements brought the man reassurance that he was looking at the right place, a brothel just north of the river in the city. The Pelican owned the brothel. He had to. The Pelican owned every brothel in the city and for three hundred miles in every direction. His interests were many, but his primary trade was skin.

A taxi pulled up in front of the brothel's entrance. A girl got out of the car and it drove away. She was talking on her phone. She wore a short skirt and looked to be in her late teens or early twenties. The man stared at her. He hadn't seen her before. Girls never went in there alone. This was new. New was good, it could mean a lead. He stood up from his crouch and watched her. He stayed close to the stairs, covered by darkness. His view of the street was better standing up. He scanned the flats up and down the street. A few yards down he saw a group of men. There were three of them. They were young, late teens probably, though they looked tough. They noticed the girl too. They watched her. The man watched them. The girl put her phone in a small hand bag and walked down the steps to the brothel.

The man's heart rate increased. 'This is something.' He thought. He considered getting closer, but thought better of it. He needed the darkness until the timing was right. With no watch, phone or clock, he counted the seconds, then minutes in his head. In less than five she came back out. She climbed the steps quickly and walked to the curb. The man swallowed saliva. He waited. She looked left and right. The man assumed she was looking for a taxi. He watched her. He saw her notice the young men on the stoop a few yards away. One of them yelled to her. The man couldn't hear what he said. He guessed it wasn't something the guy would say to his mother. The girl turned from them and started walking up the street. She pulled her phone out and put it to her ear as she walked.

The three men started walking after her, slowly at first, but as she picked up speed so did they. The man saw this. He scratched his beard hard then tapped his fist repeatedly off his thigh. He'd staked out that brothel for weeks. If he moved, he could miss his chance. Chance for what, he wasn't so sure. Night after night, same thing, same movement, same shifts, for weeks. Now the girl, the outlier. 'Fuck.' He thought. He could smell the danger she was in. Fear has an odor. Not everyone knew it, but he did. And malice has a presence. It's cold and sharp and it stings. He saw the girl turn the corner at the end of the street. The three men were closing in quickly. The man left his dark shelter and jogged across the street. When the men turned the corner, he ran to keep pace. He slowed to a walk before turning the corner himself. He peaked around it and could see the girl. She crossed the street and headed toward a large park, closed off by walls and fences. She turned and saw the men. When she turned back, she started running. The men took off after her.

The man started to run. He darted across the street. He was too far behind to catch them before they disappeared into the green. He dug in and ran as fast as he could. He reached the park gate. It was locked but there was a hole where they must have climbed through. He slid through the opening. Thorns cut his hands and tore at his heavy shirt. The girl was wrong to enter the darkness, he knew it. Fear never made decisions easier. He made it through the opening and climbed through thick bushes to a clearing. The park was quiet and empty. He heard running water from somewhere. He paused to listen. He couldn't hear much else over his heavy breathing and the heartbeat in his ears. He started to move slowly through the shadows and scanning the green as he walked. He heard a shriek. It was piercing. It

was fear incarnate. The sound echoed through the park. He guessed which direction it came from and then took off running towards it.

At first he heard nothing and he began to second guess his chosen direction. He turned down a stone path and followed it to another opening. He stumbled over the rocky ground then slipped and landed behind a row of bushes. He started to pick himself up and paused when he heard voices and what he thought was a muffled scream. He listened closely. He heard sniffling, crying held back by a forced hand. The man pulled himself to his knees and stayed low behind the row of bushes. He crawled over to where the brush was thinned and he peaked through. In a small clearing he saw the three men. One, the leader he assumed, had the girl pinned to the ground. His forearm was over her face and mouth. Another man held her hips to the ground and the third stood over the girl. A knife was in his hand.

The man watched closely. His heart was racing. Fear had set in and he'd frozen. The girl hadn't moved in seconds. He hoped he wasn't too late. He heard whispers. The man standing with the knife started to crouch down. The girl fought her hips free and kicked out at the air. The girl's fight made the

man snap to attention and he started digging around his wet knees until he was able to free a stone from the muddy ground. He got to his feet, but stayed low behind the brush. He pulled the stone back and fired it at a set of trees behind the clearing. The stone hit wood and a large crack echoed through the park. He ducked back down. Through the bushes he saw the men freeze at the noise. Then he heard whispered voices. They first looked in the direction of the trees. The man with the knife walked over towards them, while the one that held the girl's hips down got up and walked towards the brush where the man hid. The third man stayed and held the girl to the ground.

The man started to panic. Though his head intended on killing The Pelican, his heart had not yet grown accustom to the violence it would take to do so. The mud had soaked wet through to his knees and it made him cold. He felt his teeth chattering as he sat still. The noise confused the men and disrupted their plans. He wanted to keep surprise on his side for as long as he could. He dug around in the ground looking for another rock, something to defend himself with. Next to his knee he felt a sharp stone. He dug around it then moved it back and forth vigorously to shake it loose. After a moment he was able to pry it from the ground. He gripped it tightly in his hand. It was heavier than he'd hoped, but he felt he could still wield it well enough to be effective.

He got up and moved from his knees to the balls of his feet, crouched in a squat. Through the branches he could see someone approach the brush slowly. The man stood up straight and moved back to the thicker end of the bushes. He could hear the other man breathing as he moved closer. He knew a fight was inevitable, the man was inches from him. Any second he'd be found out. He took in a deep breath and held it. He watched the other man's feet move towards him, then pause, then shift towards the other direction. 'My chance.' He thought. He stood up and stepped around the bushes. He saw the man's back less than two feet away. He made a 'tst tst' noise through his teeth and the other man turned around. When he did, the man swung his arm and caught him in the jaw with the rock. A cracking sound soared through the air and the other man crumbled to the ground unconscious. The contact sent a shockwave up the man's arm and he lost the rock on the follow through. The guy holding the girl yelled and jumped to his feet. He pushed the girl back to the ground and started running towards the man. He called for his

other friend as he did. The man watched the girl roll away and then get to her feet. She made eye contact briefly and then took off running in the opposite direction.

The man turned and ran up the rocky hill that he had slid down leading back towards the clearing. He could hear shouts behind him and loud footsteps pounding off the stone and gravel path. He knew they were gaining on him. He pumped his legs as fast as he could go. His heavy boots and wet jeans held him back, but he plowed ahead and managed to reach the opening. He didn't bother maneuvering through it. He didn't slow down, he jumped up onto the tall fence and climbed up and over the bar, then jumped down to the ground. The two men following were on the fence, inches away before his boots touched down.

The man considered whether to keep running. He chose against it. The street was dark, but there was activity. A fight wouldn't go unnoticed. That made him feel safer. That feeling diminished when the first guy jumped down and pulled a knife out from his pocket. The second man jumped down and landed closer to him, dropping to his knees with the fall. The man took a quick step forward and kicked him square

in the face. He sailed backwards as blood shot from his nose. The man slid his foot back and squared himself up. The guy with the knife moved towards him. He walked slowly, circling with a tight grip on the handle. He lunged forward. The man jumped back and side-stepped the blade. He shoved the outstretched arm towards the fence, but the guy with the blade stayed on his feet and swung his knife hand back around. The man tried to jump out of the way again, but this time the blade sliced his shoulder. He felt it hit, but didn't register the pain. His thick top helped to absorb the blade's strength.

The two men squared up again. The man heard sirens in the distance. The noise was getting closer by the second. All he had to do was outlast the next attack. The man with the knife heard sirens too. They made him panic. He rushed the man again, this time looking to grab hold of him first before swinging the blade. The man slid back and let out two quick lefts to the guy's head, but the other man managed to grab hold of him anyway. The man reached the attacker's knife arm and held it back before the blade could plunge into his stomach. He shifted his feet and both men fell to the ground grappling. The man held onto the knife arm with all his strength, absorbing punches and kicks from the second man that had gotten back to his feet. He kept holding and fighting. He brought his teeth down and bit into the guy's bare wrist. He kept digging with his teeth. He heard him let out a yell. The knife finally fell from his hand. The man saw it drop and managed to kick it under the fence with his boot.

The barrage of punches and kicks stopped as the second man pulled his screaming friend to his feet. The sirens were much closer now. The two men started running down the street and turned a corner before two police cars screeched to a halt at the curb.

The man stayed on the ground, but was able to prop himself up against the fence. His adrenaline rush was wearing off and he began to feel the aches and pain of the kicks. He rubbed his shoulder, then reached into the hole in his shirt. He felt the slice. It wasn't deep, but it hurt. He took his hand out and saw blood on his fingers and palm. Two cops approached him, one tall, one chubby. Another two stood talking with people across the street, witnesses to the mayhem. The cops both crouched down. 'Are you hurt bad?' the chubby cop asked.

The man shook his head no, but winced in pain when he tried to sit up further.

'Here, can you stand?' The tall cop asked. Both reached down and helped the man stand up. 'We'll get you the hospital and get you checked out. Then we'll have some questions. That sound all right?'

The man nodded. 'That's fine. Thanks.'

They walked him over to the squad car and sat him down in the back seat with the door open. 'What's your name?' the chubby one asked.

'My name?'

'Yeah, most people have 'em, you got one?'

The man smiled. 'Of course.' His name, he hadn't thought of his name in a long time. The one he was given at birth no longer belonged to him. That man was dead. He'd never use that name again, but he hadn't thought of another one. He looked around for ideas. He saw worn ads for businesses and plays that had long since stopped running bulletined across a decaying wall. He saw an old bank's closure notice on a vacant building next to it. They all had words and letters. They meant nothing to him at all. Only two words really stood out. He used them. 'It's Grafton.' He said. 'Grafton Halifax.'

BLACKPOOL KNIGHTS (A SAMPLE)

CHAPTER 2

BENNY LUCK

Benny Luck held his hand over a pair of cards on the table and waited for the flop. Just before it came, he lifted the corners with his thumb and peaked underneath. He had a pair of sevens. His brother Randy was dealing and he began to lay down the flop, slapping each card down hard on the table making the drinks shake.

'Cool it asshole.' Benny Luck said.

'Ain't my fault you're having a shit night.' Randy said.

'No it ain't, but I don't need a drink in my lap too.'

'My table and chairs, my rules.'

'My apartment. I'll throw these plastic pieces of shit in the fireplace if I feel like it.' Benny said.

Randy flipped the last card in his hand. He placed it down slowly and then sat back in his fold out chair. Benny watched him closely for his reaction to the cards. Randy was someone that smiled and bet fast

and heavy when he had a hand. He did the same when he didn't have a hand only he did it without smiling. Benny kept his eyes on him for a few seconds. He watched him suppress it briefly, but the smile came through anyway. 'Fold.' He thought at first. He looked at the cards on the table, a two, three and a jack, not suited. Benny decided that Randy had jacks or a near straight. 'I'll stick around.' He looked at the other two guys at the table. They were the Wilson brothers, Ed and Ted. Both bruisers, he kept them around for muscle and for their loyalty, not much else. They weren't bad players though and each had a poker face like a Mongolian warlord in the cold. He had a better chance of reading mandarin than whether either of them had a good hand. Ed Wilson was first to bet and he raised. Ted matched. Randy matched, then raised again. Benny expected as much and threw his chips in to the see the turn.

Benny watched Randy's face again and saw him wince. The turn was another three and didn't seem to help anyone, though it gave Benny two pair. The Wilson brothers checked. So did Randy. Benny raised. Both Wilsons threw their cards down to fold.

'I'll see this out.' Randy said.

'I thought you might.' Benny said.

'Why's that?'

'I've never seen you fold.'

'I fold the odd time.'

'Very odd time.'

'Can't help it that I get good cards.'

'No one gets good cards that often.'

'I do.'

'You don't . . . unless you cheat.'

'Fuck you. I don't cheat.'

'I know. You gonna flip the fucking card?'

'Nah, we'll see how you like this.' Randy said. He pulled a stack of chips off his pile and dropped them into the pot.

'Why stop there? You're so confident, prove it.' Benny said. He counted up his own chips to match and slid the stack towards the center of the table. 'Well?' He asked.

Randy rubbed his hands over the top of the card deck. He stared at Benny for a few moments. Benny could tell the wheels in his head were turning. Randy looked at the chips in the pot then back to those chips in front of him. He reached for them slowly, then pulled his hand back. 'You ain't goading me Benny.'

'It doesn't look like I have to.' Benny said. 'You're thinning out yourself over there. You gonna deal or what?'

Randy pulled the card off the top of the deck, flipped it and slapped it onto the table. It was a seven. Benny smiled. He reached his hands around the pot and started pulling the chips over towards him.

'Ain't you even gonna show your cards first? You arrogant prick.' Randy said.

Benny shrugged. He turned his cards face up to show pocket sevens. 'Full house.' He said.

'Motherfucker.' Randy said.

Benny turned to the Wilsons. 'You'd think he'd learn at some point.' They both smiled and nodded. Randy stood up and walked over to the refrigerator.

'You done?' Benny yelled.

'Fuck you, yeah I'm done.'

'Get me a beer.' Benny said.

Randy disappeared behind the counter when he ducked to reach into the fridge. He came up with four beers in his arms, put them on the table and sat down. He took an opener from his pocket. He opened his own beer and then slid the opener across the table. Benny grabbed it and did the same. 'Thanks.' He said. He took a gulp from the beer. It tasted like victory after his last hand. A phone on the counter buzzed for the fifth time in ten minutes. 'That your phone buzzing?' He asked Randy.

'Yeah it is. Been going the last hour.'

'Check the damn thing. What's wrong with you?'

'I was busy taking your money off you.' Randy got up again and picked up the phone off the counter.

'How'd that work out?'

'What?'

'Taking my money. Short-lived right.'

'Yeah fuck you. Hey . . . ' Randy said. Benny looked up. He saw Randy staring into his phone, scrolling through a message.

'What's up? Who was it?'

'Text. From Dolly at the club.'

'Everything all right? You make a habit of talking to her?'

'No, that's what's odd. She said Amy was by there tonight. Looked out of it. She was looking for me . . . or us I guess.'

'Amy . . . our sister Amy?'

'Yeah. Who else?'

'At the club? How the fuck she even know about that place?'

'Come on Benny man, she's a kid, but she ain't fucking stupid. She's knows the score.'

'Try calling her.' Benny said.

Randy already had the phone to his ear. He held up his index finger. A few seconds later he took the phone from his ear. 'Straight to voicemail.' He said.

'That don't sit right.' Benny said. 'What time is it anyway?'

'It's after two am.'

'Teddy your car out front?'

'Yeah Benny.'

Benny stood up and the others did too. 'Let's take a spin by the club.' He said. The others nodded and followed him over to the door. He let the guys out then pulled the door shut tightly behind him. He checked the knob to make sure it was locked. He walked down the stairs and out the hall door to the landing. Outside it was dark and quiet. His apartment was in the city, close enough to the river that cut through its center that he could taste it on his tongue when he breathed deeply. A thin fog hung around the street lights that accented the road with a fuzzy orange. He watched from the landing as his brother and the Wilsons climbed into the car out front. He paused on the landing to think. He couldn't understand why his sister would show up at the club. The club was a brothel barely disguised. It was no place for her to be hanging around. He wished he knew her better, but he didn't. There was about ten years between them. Randy was closer to her, a few years his junior. He'd let him talk to her and figure it out. But until then he had a really bad feeling.

He pulled the zipper up on his jacket and tucked his chin underneath it. He slowly walked down the stairs, but stopped at the bottom step. He watched a slow shadow in the distance walk through the fog. Randy knocked on the window of the car to get his attention, but Benny held up his hand to hold him off. He started down the street towards the figure. It seemed small and far away. After a few steps the figure began to materialize as the blur from the fog burned off with each step. Benny heard car doors open and shut behind him as Randy and the Wilsons got out and walked after him. He saw the figure stumble and he picked up his pace, walking quickly then turning it into a jog. He heard the steps pick up behind him as the men followed. The eerie feeling he had on the steps turned to outright panic. He got closer and could see the figure was a young girl. He knew it was Amy. He ran outright towards her and got to her before she fell. Her legs were filthy and her feet were cut like she'd been running on concrete with no shoes. Her face was dirty too and she was covered

between her nose and mouth in dried blood. Benny knelt down and ran his hand through her matted hair. She didn't say anything and didn't sob, but tears began to fall from the corners of her eyes. Benny lifted her and turned towards his apartment.

'Oh shit . . . Amy?' Randy said.

'Randy, get my keys out of my jacket pocket.' Benny said. Randy reached into his pocket and found the keys. He ran ahead and opened the door. Benny struggled up the stairs carrying Amy, but he was able to make it. He pushed in through the apartment door, walked through the short hallway and over to the couch in the living room. 'No.' Amy said. 'Shower first.'

Benny knelt on the ground next to her. 'You're hurt?'

'Please Benny. Let me get clean first.'

Benny sat back on his heels. Amy managed to stand up on her own. She pointed towards a closed door next to the kitchen. Benny nodded 'yes'. 'Randy, go in my room and get some clothes, there's t-shirts and sweats and that shit in the closet.' Randy did as he was told. Amy walked slowly over to the bathroom door. She went inside and shut it behind her. Benny sat up on the couch. He leaned forward with his

elbows on his knees. Randy left clothes outside the bathroom door then came and sat in the chair across from him. 'She looks rough Benny.' Benny just nodded.

'What do you think happened to her? I'm almost afraid to ask.' Randy said.

Benny looked up at Ted and Ed Wilson. They both stayed standing with their jackets on. 'Why don't you boys hang out front for a few minutes.' Benny said. 'Randy and I gotta sort this out.' Both Wilson's nodded. Ted said, 'We'll be out front when you need us.'

'Thanks Teddy.'

Benny watched them walk out. He sat his head back on the couch and listened to the shower running. He could see Randy was nervous and upset. He was closer to Amy. He probably felt more responsible for her. Benny usually treated her with casual indifference. She was always just a little kid to him. He never liked kids. 'She don't look like a kid tonight.' He thought. 'Not anymore.' The shower stopped and the silence was deafening. He heard the door click open as Amy reached out to get the clothes Randy set for her. It shut again quickly.

'Who could've done this Benny? She's just a kid.'

'Randy, she was out very late for a kid. Plus she ain't dressed like one. Anything could've happened. Lot of bad people out there, especially in this city.' He said. Benny knew the underbelly of the city. Since the downturn Blackpool had gone the way of Gotham. He wasn't proud of it, but he knew he was part of that underbelly himself. Randy rubbed his eyes hard with the palms of his hands. Amy came out of the bathroom a couple minutes later. She slowly walked over to her brothers and sat on a wooden chair next to the couch. Benny looked at her. She looked better, but she still looked weak and definitely shaken.

'You went by the club?' Randy asked.

She nodded her head. 'I was stuck. A group of us were out. We got split up.'

'How do you know about the club?' Benny asked.

She looked at him. Her eyes were red. Benny guessed she'd been crying in the shower. 'Benny . . . everyone knows who you are. Everyone knows who all you guys are.' Benny stayed silent.

'You're a long way from home.' Randy said.

'Like I said, there was a group of us. Is this a fucking interrogation? Do you have any idea what just happened to me?'

Randy got up and walked over to her. He knelt

beside her and rested his elbow on the armrest. 'Why don't you tell us?'

Amy paused. Benny watched her. He could see on her face that whatever happened to her was too painful to relive, at least for the moment. He got up and took Randy by the arm. 'Give her time.' He whispered.

'We're sorry Amy.' Benny said. 'You're safe here kid. You hungry or something?'

'No. Just . . . tired.'

'Why don't you take my room?' He said. He pointed over to the door. 'I'm good on the couch.'

'And Randy?'

'Randy's due for a night on the floor, don't worry.'

Amy got up and headed over towards the bedroom. 'Thanks.' She said.

When she closed the bedroom door behind her Benny went over to the fridge and pulled out two beers. He opened them and handed one to Randy.

'You're not gonna find out what happened?' Randy asked.

'She'll tell us if she can Randy. She's in pain. Maybe not physically, but she's struggling. Whatever it was, it was bad. Scared her to hell.'

'You think she was . . . you know?'

'Raped?'

'You think she was?'

'I fucking hope not Randy.'

'Fuck Benny. I mean fuck. What if she was? She's a kid man. She's our sister.'

'Randy. Calm the fuck down or she'll hear you.'

'Yeah. Right. Sorry.'

'Listen. I don't know what happened, but we gotta assume from the state of her, it wasn't good. Was she raped? I don't know. Was she roughed up regardless? Definitely yes. So either way, someone's getting fucking hurt, you understand?'

'Of course I understand. How though? How we gonna find out who if we don't know what?'

'Let her sleep now Randy. She'll tell us something in the morning. In the meantime, get on the phone to O'Sullivan.'

'O'Sullivan? The cop O'Sullivan? You want to report this or something?'

'What? No. Call the fucking pig and see what was on the wires tonight. I want to know if there was any activity. She was at the club. See if any shit went down there tonight. When you're done, tell Ted and Eddy to go home, but have them head back early, like just after sunlight early. We're going hunting.'

'Okay, I'll put a call in now. What are you gonna do?'

'I'm gonna fucking lie on the couch and sleep. I need to think.'

Learn more about Paul Garvey's work by visiting paulgarveyauthor.com.

Leave a review of FIXERS at www.amazon.com/author/paulgarvey or www.goodreads.com to let other readers know what you thought.

www.ingramcontent.com/pod-product-compliance
Lightning Source LLC
Chambersburg PA
CBHW032103280326
41933CB00009B/744

* 9 7 8 1 9 4 3 4 1 5 0 1 4 *